A

HISTORY

OF THE

UPPER COUNTRY

OF

SOUTH CAROLINA

FROM THE

EARLIEST PERIODS

TO THE

CLOSE OF THE WAR OF INDEPENDENCE

BY

JOHN H. LOGAN, A.M.

VOL. II

A JOURNAL OF PERSONALITIES,
REMINISCENCES, TRADITIONS
AND HISTORY OF THE REVOLUTION
IN SOUTH CAROLINA

Copyright © 1980 by:

The Rev. Silas Emmett Lucas, Jr.

All rights reserved. No part of this publication may be reproduced, stored in a retrieval system or transmitted in any form or by any means without the prior written permission of the publisher.

Please Direct All Correspondence and Book Orders to:

Southern Historical Press, Inc.
PO Box 1267
375 West Broad Street
Greenville, SC 29602-1267
or
southernhistoricalpress@gmail.com

----

southernhistoricalpress.com

ISBN #0-89308-195-7

Printed in the United States of America

LOGAN MANUSCRIPT.

This manuscript was secured at great expense by Mrs. Thomas M. Green of Washington, Wilkes Co., Ga., who has kindly permitted us to use extracts. These extracts include all names in what was intended to be Vol. II of Logan's History of Upper Carolina, but which is now published for the first time.

This manuscript of Part 2 of Dr. Logan's History of the Upper Carolina was first published in 1910 as an addition to The Historical Collections of the Joseph Habersham Chapter of the DAR, Volume 3. However, they neglected to include mention of this manuscript in the Table of Contents of that volume.

As Publisher of the reprint edition of Volume 3 just described I have felt that this manuscript needed wider circulation, especially during this period in which we celebrate our nation's Bicentennial, and therefore am issuing it as a separate title with a newly prepared full name index.

Note corrections in spelling of names: Finsley should be Tinsley, McFunkin should be McJunkin, Gouldelock should be Goudelock.

LOGAN MANUSCRIPT.

(From manuscript of Dr. John H. Logan, collected with a view of writing a second volume of His History of the Upper Country of South Carolina, of which he had published Volume I in 1859, and which the subsequent civil war prevented the completion. Dr. Logan then residing at Greenwood, Abbeville district or county, S. C., but since removed to Talladega, Alabama. The manuscript, however, was left in charge of Dr. E. R. Calhoun, his father-in-law, of Greenwood.—L. C. D.)

Statement of Robert Long, of Laurens District, S. C., made evidently in 1843: Born in Antriver country, Ireland, about first April, 1763, brought first to Pennsylvania in his infancy, and at about 27 years old to where he now lives.

That being under age he did no military duty till the 15th April, 1778, when he volunteered on horseback under Capt. Josiah Greer, of the Little River regiment of South Carolina militia, otherwise Col. James Williams. Capt. Thos. Dugan's company of same regiment and Capt. Greer were ordered by Col. Williams over Saluda after some tories who had set off for East Florida to join the King's people; after crossing Saluda and going as far as the Piney Woods Hosue, they returned to Col. Williams' plantation, when Lieut. Col. Robert McCrery, of same regiment, took the command, and Capt. Benj. Kilgore's and Capt. Robert Ritchey's company joined us. Ritchey's lieutenant was Richard Golding, Kilgore's lieutenant was John D. Cue, Dugan's, Levi Casey, and Green's, Matthew McCrery and Jas. McNees. Lockley Leonard was adjutant; James Dillard, Sergeant Major, and Charles Smith, Quartermaster. After crossing Saluda and Savannah rivers, we then joined Brig. Gen. A. Williamson; his staff, Benj. Crafton, Adjutant-General, as he was called, _____ Purves, Major of Brigade, John E. Calhoun, Wagon-Master General, etc.

The object of this campaign was to take St. Augustine. We crossed Ogeechee, at Gov. Wright's plantation, and he forded at the precise time of the notable eclipse of the sun, 24th June. July 4th over Cat Head Swamp had 13 guns fired there for independence; 2 or 3 days after, crossed the Altamaha river, then Little Satilla and Great Satilla, then St. Mary's. Gen'l. Robert Howe, of the Continentals, with 3 or 4 regiments of South Carolina regulars were there, as also Gov. John Houston, Georgia. His army was composed of regulars, minute men and militia.

Gen'l. Williamson's army consisted of Col. Hammond's regiment commanded by himself and Maj. Pickens; Col. (John) Winn's, commanded by himself; Col. Goodwin's, the same; Col. Thomas' regiment commanded by Maj. Thomas Brandon; Col. Lyle's by himself, and Williams as above, amounting, as was said, to 1,200 men. Had no fighting except that Col. Clark did at Brown's Battery on Alligator Swamp. Major Pickens was sent there with 500 men. Brown was gone. A council of war was called, and they determined to return home, where we arrived 14th August, being about four months out.

The next time he volunteered against Col. Boyd of the Tories, under same Captain J. Greer and Lieut. McCrery; Lieut. Col. McCrery and Maj. John Williams of said regiment, and Major Thomas Brandon of Thomas' regiment. Having heard of a refractory spirit North (of) Enoree river, in now Spartanburg, Maj. Brandon and Capt. Palmer had been sent with 30 men to allay it, but the Tories were then too numerous for them. Capt. Greer, having notice, raised 30 men to reinforce them, of whom he was one, when there was found that they amounted to 500. We got reinforced to about 250 in two or three days, and pursued after them, crossing Saluda, Little River and Rocky river to Savannah river. Col. Pickens defeated them in Georgia. Set out about the 7th of January, 1779, and got home about the 13th February—37 days on horseback.

On a two months tour on foot, in 1779, 1st June to last of July, 61 days, under Capt. Joseph Greer commanded by Maj. Robert Gillam of same 'regiment, Capts. Charles Saxon, Wm. Milner; Hugh Saxon, Adjutant; Robert Ross, Sergeant Major; George Neely, Commissary, against the British at Stone in South Carolina, crossed Saluda and some forks of Edisto, 2 months.

August 10th, 1779, against the Creek Indians same regiment and company officers, and Brigadier A. Williamson and Col. Andrew Pickens, crossed Saluda, Little river, Rocky river and Savannah river. Got home 8th October—58 or 59 days out on horseback. The object was to take a certain Cameron, superintendent for the British over the Cherokee Indians, then at the Big Shoemake, in the Creek Nation. Cameron, having got notice of their object, slipped out of the way, supposed by Gen. Williamson, then a traitor.

March 1st to June 7th, 1780, under Capt. Joseph Greer, Lieut. Virgin, and Lieut. Col. R. McCrery; Robt. Ross, Sergeant Major; Joshua Picke(n)s, Quartermaster; Capts. Saxon, Milner, and Stevens,—crossed Saluda and Savannah rivers; lay in camp 2 miles South of Augusta six or seven weeks at the time of the siege of Charleston, then crossed Savannah with 138 men to go to the siege. Joined Col. A. Pickens near the Ridge, Major Noble of the line, and Major Bowie of brigade, the whole of the command amunting to about 300 men. Charleston having surrendered, crossed Congaree river, went up to Camden, then home 7th of June, crossing Broad river. Col. McCrery surrendered to the Tories with Capt. Greer's company of 30 men.

November 3rd, 1780, he escaped as a refugee from the British and Tories, and joined the American army under Gen. Thomas Sumpter; served on horseback in the fragment of the Little River regiment then commanded (after Col. J. Williams' death) by Col. Joseph Hayes and in the company formerly commanded by Capt. Greer, but now by Capt. Sam'l. Swing and Lieut. James Dillard.

When Sumter had crossed the Enoree, he went to take a view of Col. Tarleton's camp at Sherer's Ferry on Broad river; immediately on his return to his former camp, he odered Ewing's company of 14 men to cross Dunkin's creek, and reconnoitre the country towards the fort the Tories had on Col. Williams' plantation; and upon our returning to Sumter's camp, he had decamped, having gotten certain notice that Tarlton was advancing upon him. We followed Sumter's trail, crossing Enoree, found Tarlton was between us and Sumter; took two of his men and escaped. This is the reason we were not in the battle of Blackstocks. Crossed the Tyger Fair forest, and joined Col. Brandon next day, and took a number of prisoners and came up with our prisoners to Sumter's camp on Pacolet at Buffenton'd Iron Works, then crossed Pacolet to Gondelock's; from there Col. Lacey, Col. Tyles, Col. Hayes, Col. Bratton, Lieut. Col. Nixon, and Major Fair, with about 100 men, were sent across Pacolet, down Broad river near the British camp, near which had a skirmish with 'em in the night; Col. Nixon was killed and two or three others on our part. Crossed the Tyger and Broad rivers that night, and Sandy river next day, and on to Col. Watson's, near Hill's Iron Works. In a few days marched to Love's Ford on Broad river—that is, Capts. Casey, Ewing and Harris, commanded by Col. Hayes; joined Col. Brandon there; from that to 3rd or 4th December lay by not a day,—no, nor night either, but marching and counter-marching, occasionally crossing and re-crossing Broad river, Pacolet, Tyger, and Enoree,— sometimes Cols. Brandon and Hayes together, at others detached in companies as the service seemed to require, or as the enemy receded or advanced. 3rd or 4th December at night at Holanswith's Mill near Broad river, Col. Hayes with Capts. Casey, Ewing and Harris of his own regiment, and Capt. Blasangam of Col. Brandon's, about 40 men, crossed the Tyger and Enoree next day, and by next night rode near 40 or 50 miles to Col. Dugan's place; at dark attacked Major Lantrip with about 60 Tories; wounded 8 and took 10 prisoners. Col. Hayes, and Capts. Harris and Blassengam, Capt. Casey, and Capt. Ewing, re-crossed Enoree, Tyger and Broad rivers, about 20th December; again on 24th crossed Pacolet in the night, Grindal's Shoal; 25th Gen. Morgan joined us with 500 men; 26th Col. W(ashington's) cavalry, 84 (in number); and 27th at sunset crossed Pacolet. Col. Washington's 84 cavalry, and Cols. Brandon and Hayes about 200 militia, rode that night about 16 miles, and next day about after crossing Tyger and Enoree, attacked Col. Moore and about 500 Tories on Bush river; killed and wounded a great many, took 40 or 50 prisoners, and dispersed the rest and also Will Cunningham, with 100 more a mile or two from Moore's camp; and on the next day the fort at Williams' plantation. On our return to Gen. Morgan's, South of Enoree, met Cols. Thomas and Roebuck with 200 men, and just on the North of it, met Col. A. Pickens just escaped from the Tories at Ninety-Six, and 95 men with him. Crossing the Enoree, Tyger and Pacolet got to Morgan's camp. Provisions and forage being scarce in that part; Pickens about that time advanced to command the brigade, crossed the Pacolet with his own, Col. Brandon's and Hayes' regiments, and moved down Fairforest as a body of observation, and to encourage our friends to turn out, which they did then considerably after Moore's defeat.

January 12th, 1781, Pickens at Fairforest meeting house got notice from his spies that Tarleton was advancing fast towards Morgan's camp. We crossed Fairforest at dark, and Pacolet at Skal Shoal, 16 miles, then marched to Morgan's camp 8 miles. On hearing Pickens' relation, Morgan beat a retreat. Marched up the road towards Cowpens, and Pickens up Pacolet through the hills; camped that night, the 13th, on a very high hill. 14th joined Morgan, camped together that night, Cols. Thomas and Roebuck also with 200 men; 15th passed Brushfort on Mickelty; 16th marched close order all day till in the night; set the woods on fire in two or three places, which no doubt retarded Tarleton's pursuit each time at least a fourth of an hour; which brought sun up before he was in sight of us.

The 17th (January) the infantry marched out in sections, and divided two and two as they got ten paces of Hayes' regiment already formed across the road. Hayes regiment then moved to the right of the infantry, 70 or 80 yards in advance; Major McDowell, of North Carolina, in advance of us 70 or 80 yards, and Major Triplet, of Virginia, in our rear; Cols. Thomas and Roebuck in the extreme right. The left wing was similarly formed of militia. The cavalry in rear of infantry. The watch-word was on being hailed, viz.: "Who are you?" Answer: "Fire." Reply, "Sword." So the word was fire and sword. By this we were to know our friends from foes.

Hayes' regiment having advanced too far were to retreat and form on our old ground; when the North Carolinians were retreating in order to be ready to cover their retreat; failing of this the Virginians broke before we got to them. We were not rallied until Gen. Morgan did it in person. At that time Tarleton brought 200 or 300 cavalry round in the rear of our left wing of militia. Col. Washington charged them with his cavalry; at the same time our infantry charged the British with the bayonet, and took their field pieces, while those on the right and left surrendered or retreated.

Crossed Broad river next day, and on to Gilbert Town, where we left the arms taken from the British. General Pickens with the militia, took the prisoners through the spur of the mountains; and Gen. Morgan with the infantry and cavalry pushed on for Ransom's Mill, South fork, and Sherard's Ford, on Main Catawba, where he crossed. The British crossing in a few days, particularly the first day of February, Morgan crossed the Gadkin.

Immediately before Tarleton's defeat, A. Pickens was made Brigadier-General, and James Jackson his Major of Brigade; Capt. Levi Casey Lieut. Col. under Col. J. Hayes, Jared Smith his Major, and James Dillard, Lieut. under Capt. Ewing. Under Capt. Ewing (Lomg) continued to serve with Pickens and Morgan till about the time they crossed the Dan, and till 1st April, 1781, (except while in on small-pox). Being then destitute of every clothing, had to quit the service, and to work to obtain clothing; from that, and a long, tedious and severe sickness, he did not get back to South Carolina till 1st March, 1782.

He then entered under Capt. James Dillard of the aforesaid company (Capt. Ewing having resigned) he succeeded him, John Jones was Lieut. under him in said company.

Cols. Hayes being killed by Will Cunningham and the Tories, Levi Casey was Colonel, Jared Smith Lieut. Colonel, and Thomas Dugan Major. Under and with the above officers he served till in February, 1783.

The last service he did was under Lieut. Jones, of said company, after a company of Tories who were making an incursion into the Little River regiment, but they went off before we got up with them. This service, namely from the 1st of March, 1782, 'till in February, 1783, he can give no particular account of, as sometimes he served $\frac{1}{2}$, and other $\frac{1}{3}$, and some but $\frac{1}{4}$ of his time, just as circumstances required. However, he has no doubt in saying that he served at least one-third of that time. (End.)

This was made to secure a pension. L. C. D.

COL. BRATTON.—Col. Bratton came with his father from Antrim, Ireland, first to York County, Pa., and then to Virginia, where he married a Miss Robertson, and afterwards removed to York, District, S. C., and settled where Mrs. Bratton, his daughter-in-law, now lives, some 10 miles from Yorkville.

KING'S MOUNTAIN.—This battle was fought on Saturday Next morning they hung several Tories just above Ferguson's Markee, and left them hanging. The poor fellows begged hard for their lives. In 1840 some men opened the grave, and found the skeleton of a man, and by his side a long knife. Virginia Sal, a red-headed woman Ferguson had brought from Virginia, was killed, and buried in the same grave with Ferguson. Numerous buttons have been found marked "R. P." —Royal Protection,—belonging to Tories.

The Rock under the oak was under Ferguson's Markee, and was used by him as a sort of chair, and perhaps as a table.

WM. CARSON was in this battle,—he was with Hamright.

WM. BRATTON, when about 18, and studying medicine, took up Hank's body, and made a skeleton of it as far as it remained,—this was taken by a member of the family to Alabama, where it is still.

Memos.—See an ancient book in the hands of Dr. Howe in relation to the early settlement and condition of the upper country.

See an old book in the possession of Wm. Rosser, of Camden, in relation to Smith, the McCords and Fort Motte.

COL. RHD. WINN lies buried in a lonely brier thicket, near Williamsport, Tennessee.

Memo.—Don't forget John Simonton and the Tory killed near the residence of David Wilson. They were going with prisoners to Ninety Six,—one of them was shot there and buried on the spot." 1857.

Memo.—Wm. Dickson's father was a Major under McClure at Hook's defeat—he lived at Walker's Cross Road, on the old Nation ford road, in East Chester. 1857.

FISH DAM FORD.—Col. Tom Taylor led at Fish Dam Ford. Weyniss led the Tories. He approached the camp at night. "Boys," said Taylor, "give them a little powder at first—draw them from the fires, and when they are between them and you, then chuck them."

Memo.—See B. R. Campbell for manuscript in the Lodge at Laurens, once in the hands of Maj. Barksdale.—1857.

Memo.—Pat Calhoun, son of Wm. Calhoun and Agnes Long, born Feb. 18, 1760.

AGE OF TREES.—A chestnut 2 feet across the stump is something more than 80 years; a pine 2 feet across the stump is

180 years; an oak 1½ feet acrss th stump, about 40 years. 1857.

"The Onion," Pubd. at Athens and Penfield.

The Magnolia, Charleston, by Pendleton, Burgess and James.

Memo.—"Many of Gen. (Wm.) Butler's papers are in the Pension Office, Washington City." 1857.

"Glover hung on Fairforest for killing Burgess."

See Mr. T. O. P. Vernon (Lancaster, S. C.) for manuscripts and an old book of sketches.—1857.

GEN. ROBERT IRWIN, N. C., writes to his brother, Capt. John Irwin, near Ninety Six, S. C., June 5th, 1781, saying that he is to set off next week for the Assembly; that his brother Alex'r., died about a year ago; his estate yet unsettled; wish you wd. come in this Fall and I wd. settle for you if empowered. Sorry to hear of the much distressed condition of things in Ninety-Six region, etc.

SAMUEL IRWIN, another brother, writes from Carlisle, Cumberland Co., Pa., Oct, 1st, 1792, to his brother John Irwin, near Ninety Six, S. C. Hence it is quite certain Gen. Robert Irwin was originally from Cumberland Co., Pa.

—KING'S MOUNTAIN BATTLE—

Robert C. Gillam, Asheville, N. C., Sept. 29th, 1858, to Dr. J. H. Logan:

"I have called to see Mr. Robert Henry at your request, and have taken down what he says about the Battle of King's Mountain. After reading Ramsey's account of it in his *Annals of Tennessee,* I do not think what he details as his knowledge and acts in the battle of material moment.

He says that he was thirteen years of age (the figures *very plain*—L. C. D.), and joined in with the over-mountain men under Col. Chronicle with 20 other recruits, at Probert's place on Broad River. He went into the action with, and was (near) by Chronicle, when he was shot. They surrounded

Ferguson, and charged up the mountain. Early in the engagement he was run through by a British bayonet, tumbled over a log and lay still, until all was over. They charged over him two or three times in the attacks and retreats of regulars, but he kept dark until he was relieved by a friend, who pulled out the bayonet and let him up. He had shot the British soldier who transfixed him, but was not able to free himself of the bayonet.

"He says Shelby accused Campbell of cowardice, but he thinks Shelby was wrong, and it is probable that he mistook him for Graham, as they both rode black horses, and that Graham was known to be a coward.

"Knows nothing of Williams more than that he was wounded on the field and died a few days after.

"No Tories were hanged on the field of battle. They (the Whigs) lay on the ground Saturday night. On Monday they hanged nine at Walker's.

Knows nothing of Lacey, or anything further of the battle of King's Mountain.

See E. C. McLure's letter, Dec. 8, 1873, for more about *Mr. Henry.*—L. C. D.

LAUDON WATERS, grandson of a brother of Col. Phil. Waters, shortly after the battle of Entau entered the army with his father, Boardwine Waters; and about this time the latter got a parole, with eleven other men, to visit their families in Newberry. John Clark and Laudon Waters were two of the number. On their return back to the American army at Ninety Six (then this must have been *before* Entau battle,—L. C. D.), in travelling a circuitous route, B. Waters ordered John Clark and Laudon Waters in advance of his command as spies, and cautioned them if they saw men to return to him. In passing round a precipice which was caused by a branch entering the river, Ned Turner, the out-lawyer, with a scout of about twenty Tories in this valley (evidently in Spartanburg District, about a mile from Musgrove's Mill,—L. C. D.) of the river, captured John Clark and Laudon Waters, upon which B. Waters came up immediately, when his command fled and left him alone. Upon which he, (B. Waters) drew his arms and parleyed with Ned Turner for the release of Clark and L. Waters; upon which Turner and four others advanced, and ordered him to surrender,—when Waters grounded his arms.—Ned Turner at this shot him dead. The Tories came up and robbed him of his armor and horse. Turner and his party then took up their march in a pine country with his prisoners, Clark and young Waters, a distance of about 4 miles, and then turned my father loose to return and bury his father. He went home, and with his mother and some other ladies, buried him upon the ground where he lay; 4 years after he was taken up and buried at Bush river church in Newberry, where his remains now lie. Many years after this Ned Turner, the out-law, returned to Newberry during my recollection, and John Clark by chance was informed that Turner was in this neighborhood secreted at a certain house,— went and as Turner emerged upon the door steps next morning, Clark shot him through the chest, and Turner fell bleeding, and Clark left. Turner's friends had a coffin made, and filled with some refuse, and buried in the garden, pretending that he died; while in fact he was removed to another neighbor's house, and finally recovered, and left the country. When it was rumored that Turner was not killed, Clark exhumed the coffin, and learned the ruse practiced on him. No more of Ned Turner until 1832, when he died in Florida in his 86th year.

Laudon Waters died in 1822, and was buried in the family graveyard, a mile from Musgrove's Mill.

P. M. Waters (son of Laudon), who writes the preceding, says further of his grandfather, Boardwine Waters, brother of Col. Phil. Waters, a native of Virginia, and early settled in Newberry District, had occasion to go down to Dutch Ford on business, after times became troublesome; and on his return found to his surprise one of his neighbors, together with the grocery keeper and two others,—who were in favor of the King; this neighbor, under the influence of liquor, insisted on

B. Waters subscribing an oath of allegiance to the King, which he refused to do,—upon which they came to words. Waters in the act of starting for home walked out of the grocery, when this neighbor seized a loaded rifle, which stood in the corner of the grocery, and pursued Waters, and presenting the gun, saying: "I will kill you unless you subscribe to the oath." Waters then commenced parleying with him, and by stratagem snatched the gun from him, and turned it upon him. When the fellow seized a stick and turned upon Waters,—who gave back, and bid him stand off or he would kill him,—and finally shot him and he died immediately. Consulting with his brother, Col. Phil Waters, B. Waters, surrendered himself to the civil authorities, and was put in Ninety Six jail. Not long after, Col. P. Waters and friends liberated him by cutting down the door in a dark night—upon which B. Waters left immediately and took refuge in the North, and there joined the American army; and returning South with Green, fought at Entau Springs.

Another memo. speaks of the affair at Ninety Six when Cunningham commanded the Scofielites, and attacked Col. Williamson,—formerly voer 3,000,—latter scarce 500; 5 swivels carrying one and a half pound balls; only one Whig killed in the three days Tory firing. This statement by Robt. Long, of Laurents County, S. C.

ROBERT LONG'S MEMOS.—After Blackstock's Battle, he was in a skirmish under Col. Lacey, at the mouth of Tyger River; and afterwards in another under Col. Joseph Hayes, at Col. Dugan's; then at Col. Moore's, of the Tories, defeat, on Bush river, under Col. Washington; and next day under Col. Hayes at the taking of the fort from the Tories at Col. Williams'."

Another memo.—June, 1776, the Cherokees fell on the frontiers, assisted by some of the Tory refugees, who had fled to them in December, 1775, when Richardson suppressed their insurrection in Ninety Six region,—murdered a number of families, and attacked Lindley's Fort, but were repelled and defeated, and sued for peace.

ROBERT LONG'S ACCOUNT OF COL. SAM'L HAMMOND'S SERVICES:

States on oath that he was acquainted with S. H. in the Rev. War, and more particularly after the reduction of Charleston,—about the 1st of July, he saw him in Laurens Dist. in command of a small company of men on his way to join the Northern army; that he stopped 2 or 3 days in bounds of the Dunkin's Creek company of the old Little river reg't of militia, to give time for some Whigs to prepare to go on with him,—in which time he piloted 4 to his company, this was just before the fight at Musgrove's Mill, which he must have been in; that some time after he saw him (Sam'l. Hammond) in General Sumter's camp; that he must have been with Sumter in the fight at Blackstock's.

You passed as Captain on Friday night before the fight at Blackstock's—you came with your company to John Odle's on Enoree, and went with us into Sumter's camp at John Smith's just as Sumter returned from Therer's Ferry. Fourteen of us under Capt. Ewing were sent out to reconnoitre towards Williams' Fort; when we returned Sumter had retreated towards Blackstock's, and Tarleton between us and Sumter. We knew nothing of this till we came up with Tarleton's rear and took two of his men prisoners.

Capt. Inman, James Dillard and Isaac Greer were sent by General Morgan in the night before the fight at Cowpens to notice Tarleton's approach, etc.

(Now resume deposition of R. Long's.)

That deponent knows that Capt. Hammond was in Tarleton's defeat, but thinks he was then promoted to Major; thinks he commanded on the left wing front line, and this deponent was under Col. Jo. Hayes, next to Col. Howard's infantry; that he saw him afterwards both in South and North Carolina with Gen. Pickens till, he was attached as a Major, or Captain to Gen. Sumter's State troops or cavalry.

Adds that he sends the deposition of James Dillard, Sen'r., also of Laurens.—No date, except elsewhere on the paper has the year "1832" on it.—L. C. D.

These MSS. of Robert Long were sent to Dr. Logan, by D. C. Long, only surviving son of Robert, June 10, 1858,—of Dallas Co., Ala., P. O. Uniontown, Parry County, Alabama

Dr. Thos. Weir, of Laurens, S. C., is a brother-in-law.

From late PHILIP EDWARD PEARSON'S (of Matagorda, Texas) Manuscript History of Fairfield District, S. C.,—a native of Fairfield District, an eminent lawyer, and for many years solicitor of the District. He took great interest in everything connected with the Colonial and Revolutionary history of S. C., and his memory was a perfect storehouse of facts, incidents, etc.

EXTRACTS.

CRAVEN COUNTY.—The District of country known as Fairfield, in South Carolina, was in early times an undivided part of Craven County, and Parish of St. Mark's. The County and the Parish, which were identical in limits, were three times as large as the present Alabama, extending from tide water in Carolina to the Mississippi river.

THE CATAWBAS.—The Catawbas, says tradition, were originally from the neighborhood of Montreal. The French and Carmewaugas owed them most deadly hatred. Determining to escape their powerful adversaries, they crossed the St. Lawrence, probably at Detroit, and moved on Southwest with their best speed. The Carmewaugas gave them chase, and on the upper streams of the Kentucky (called in some old maps Katawba) came up with the fugitives. Making a virtue, an da noble one, of necessity, the gallant Catawbas turned upon their pursuers, and gave them a terrible overthrow. It was an Indian Hohenlinden. At this point the little nation divided. One division took their way for the Mississippi, and was most probably absorbed in the greater tribes of Chickasaws or Choctaws. About 1825, the steam-boat Catawba arrived from the West at Mobile, and it was said she was called after some stream in the far Southwest. The other division turned from their battle-ground to the East, and settled for some years on Catawba Creek, Bottetourt County, Virginia. This division afterwards moved on South to Catawba river, in South Carolina, where they encountered the jealous but magnanimous Cherokees,—arriving in Carolina about 1650. Ramsey in his History of South Carolina, makes a solemn appeal to the people to foster the remnant of that most deserving and magnanimous tribe. How far this suggestion has been attended to, Carolinians may answer. The Catawbas never did shed one drop of white men's blood. It is true, they were crusty when the whites made their first encroachments upon the Catawba lands, but they were soon easily pacified. * * * South Carolina never fell into any difficulty in which she did not find the Catawbas by her side. A company was with Barnwell in his expedition against the Tuscaroras; another was with Rhett, the year after; another with Col. Thomson (the old Ranger) when the British on Long Island threatened the rear of Fort Moultrie; another with Williamson, and afterwards with Pickens, in the Cherokee War, and always brave and faithful.

Gen'l. New River, Old Scott and Catawba George were renowned warriors * * * The Catawbas were as remarkable for their honesty as for their bravery. A party of them were accused of taking corn from a settler's crib on Toole's Fork of Fishing Creek. They repelled the charge indignantly, saying: "All is lost but our honor." During the Revolutionary War the smallpox took off hundreds of Catawbas; and in after times fire-water precipitated their destiny. In 1835, the noble little nation numbered about one hundred of poor dispirited people, suffering for the commonest necessaries of life. The Indian can not work. He has with all the colored races throughout the world a lack of foresight and perseverance, and when brought into contact with the Anglo-Saxon race perish he must.

A reconciliation was apparently effected between the Catawbas and their Northern enemies about 1760, at Albany. The Catawba King and six of his warriors accompanied Lieut. Gov. Bull to that city, where Royal Governors and Indian Chiefs were appointed to meet for a general pacification. Mr. Bull had the precaution to keep his Catawba friends closely concealed in the hotel until it could be ascertained whether the Connewaugas would bury the hatchet with them or not. They said for some time that they never would be friends with the Catawbas, whilst the grass grew or the water ran. With much persuasion they at length relented, and then Mr. Bull brought out his Catawbas. The King and his warriors advanced toward the place of meeting with the rim of their caps down, and chanting a national song. On approaching the house, they threw up the rim of their caps, ceased their solemn melody, entered the house with a firm step and took the place assigned. They were admired by the white men as well as by the red, for their extraordinary grace and dignity. A universal peace was the result of the meeting. This narrative of the Albany meeting is taken from Mr. Bull's beautiful and graphic letter to the Colonial Government, recorded in the Indian Book preserved in the Secretary of State's Office at Columbia.

The assassination of King Hagler was a dreadful shock to the Catawbas, from which they never recovered. About 1766, seven Shawnees secretly invaded the Catawba territory. The old King was residing some distance from the chief town, to allow his young men a better chance to hunt, and his women to manufacture pottery. His country residence was a sort of Sans Souci. The lurking Shawnees picked the opportunity and murdered the venerable and most beloved chieftain. The fatal news was immediately conveyed to the town, and pursuit in no time commenced after the wrong-doers. Six of them were tracked out by an unbarking dog, and captured. The seventh made his escape by swimming the river. Arriving in safety on the western (shore), he flourished the scalp of old Hagler in barbarous triumph.

A tragedy deeper than ever described followed. In the Catawba council the six captives were sentenced to death by whipping. As all work but hunting and war was assigned to the women, so the women on this dreadful occasion were appointed the executioners. One after another the captives were pinioned by one hand to a stake. The victim was furnished with a small (   ) containing pebbles. So soon as the lash was applied, he commenced rattling his gourd, and chanting his death song. Life lasted under this flagellation from sun-rise to sun-set. When the sixth Shawnee was tied to the stake, and the female furies were about to commence their infernal operation, a beautiful Catawba girl named Bettie rushed in to his rescue. She said she loved him, and claimed him for her husband. The occurrence struck all present forcibly. A council was immediately called to determine on what was proper to be done on an occasion so novel—and interesting. The council said that in an ordinary case the claim of Betty would have all its effect, but the crime charged on the prisoner, the killing of the King, was altogether unpardonable. They decided that the sentence of death should be forthwith executed. The executioners were about addressing themselves to the work of death. Betty rushed in a second time, and with a hatchet clove his skull, and he fell dead instantly. She declared aloud that if she could not have him for her husband, the nation should not have the satisfaction of seeing his bleeding body torn by the scourge. Betty afterwards married an Indian of the name of Jackson; but in her extreme old age, when her beloved Shawnee was alluded to, she said with great feeling that she "loved him too much." Such is the inexhaustible wealth of the genuine female heart.

REVOLUTIONARY WAR.—Fairfield was not a battle-field. It was remarked that many of the Whigs established a fair fame for heroism. Sumter said Benjamin May was the bravest man he ever knew. Among the Tories not one hero was to be found. The Whigs and Tories met at Mobley's Meeting House, and after the first crack of the rifle the Tories fled to a man. The same thing occurred at a Whig and Tory skirmish at Caldwell's place, on Lee's Creek, and after the firing and rout of the Tories perfect, their leader Col. John Phillips was found squatted in a brier patch, and dragged out a prisoner. The court of appeals of South Carolina has tacitly affirmed the doctrine that the devil is entitled to his due. And according to that decision, John Phillips was entitled to his due. He had an unaccountable influence over Cornwallis, and in the beneficent exercise of that influenec he obtained pardon for all the Whigs condemned to death at the drum-head court, whilst his Lordship occupied Winnsboro. During the stay of the British he often sent for John Milling and Watty Robertson to converse with him about matters connected with his command. Cornwallis ordered the country people to be paid liberally for their produce, and molested no one in the enjoyment of civil rights. With due military ceremonies and precautions he admitted every one to his markee who chose to call.

John Mills, of Chester, gained admission to the markee. "And who," said Cornwallis, "are you?" "My Lord," replied Mills, "do no you remember ould John Mills who kept your father's race-horses in Ireland?" "Oh, is that you, John? Give us a wag of your bone, and help yourself right freely to spirits and water." John drank but failed to grace his draw with a toast. "And have you any business with me, my old friend?" "Yes, your Lordship. I understand you have it in view to hang a good many of your dam't Whigs, and I had it in mind say till ye, that that was not the way to succeed with these people. Besides, nothing is more uncertain than the fate of battles, and your Lordship and your brave men may change places with the Whigs now condemned to die. My son John is one of the damndest Whigs in the colony, and if your Lordship goes on to hang, and you should afterwards fall into John's hands, he would hang up your Lordship like a dog." Johnny's speech had its possible effect,—for nobody was hung, no property plundered or destroyed.

It would not be worth while to speak of the spirited attack made by part of Sumter's force on the British post at Rocky Mount. Turnbull, in command of that post with British and

Tories, made out to maintain his position with inconsiderable loss. The hope in the attack consisted in firing a stack of hay, and so communicating the flame to the fort. But the unruly wind blew the wrong way. And how often in life do we find that we fail because the wind is perverse or intractable? James Johnston, commonly known as Adjutant Johnston, was the Whig hero on this occasion. He wore then the blade which graced the side of his grand-father at the siege of Deny.

After the defeat of the British at Blackstock's, the wreck of the British troops engaged in that fight dropped down to Mrs. Dansby's near Broad river. The poor old widow was forthwith ordered out of the dwelling with her children. She refused to go; force was threatened. She bid defiance to force. "I will not say what I am; but *you* say I am a British subject, and if so, I have the rights of a British subject until I am legally divested by the verdict of a jury. If you must needs have a shelter, go take the kitchen, and make the best of it." They took her at her word, and British officers, scarlet-clad, and trimmed off with gold lace, and decorated with gold epaulettes, were glad to find an asylum in poor old Martha Dansby's kitchen. Such is the effect of indomitable resolution exerted in the right spirit, in a good cause. Many of the British officers and soldiers wounded at Blackstock's died here. Among the rest, and chiefest in all that constitutes the man and the hero was Major Money. He was connected with some of the highest names in old England, and distinguished for scholarship, kind-heartedness and gallantry. The day he was summoned from the kitchen to another world, the pewter on the shelf rattled with the excess of his convulsive agonies, and he cried out often: "Come on, brave boys. We value none of them but Tom Sumter and Will Washington."

Major Money is particularly mentioned, because, strange to say, his English friends were never apprised of his fate, and not thirty years ago inquiries were made after him. He sleeps on the hill-top where he breathed his last, and the winds have long since whispered his requiem.

Besides contributing many brave men to the regiment of Rangers (Col. Thomson's,—Capt. Woodward's company) afterwards to Sumter's, and sometimes to Marion, Fairfield sustained the great cause with a noble spirit.

After the drawn battle of Hobkirk Hill, which the British claimed as a victory, Greene passed over the Wateree at Grave's Ford, and encamped on the N. bank of Sawny's creek. His vigilant adversary, Rawdon, crossed the Wateree at Camden, and marching up encamped on the south side of that stream. The creek was not large, but the banks were high, steep and impracticable. Here the two armies met face to face, and both concluded to retire without a battle. Rawdon dropped down towards the low country; and Greene with his wretched force, almost naked, swarming with vermin, thinned by two battles, and scrawny with famine, took post at Mr. Reuben Harrison's. They needed everything. They tented under the blue arch of kind reaven, slackened nothing of purposes and resolve, and looked manfully forward to happier times and brighter days. Mr. Harrison had been with Sumter in his perils, his partial successes, and his defeats. He thought like a soldier, and he felt like a man. He ordered his people to forward to the army breadstuffs, vegetables, fat cattle and fat sheep in plenty. Greene remained at his bivouac for a whole week, living on the hospitality of Mr. Harrison. When about to march, having no strong box, he tendered to his host a certificate for the bountiful supplies he had furnished. "No," said Harrison, "we are all engaged in the same great cause. You are welcome to all you have received. Your success will be my pay."

In one of his marches through the uplands, Washington's corps of cavalry halted at Ingleman's Mill, on Wilkinson's creek, sometimes called Owen's creek. His object probably was to watch the motions of the British Col. Junes, who was posted at Scheerer's Ferry (afterwards called Strother's, afterwards Clap's,) Washington was out of money and supplies. The commissary, Mr. Hutchinson, was sent over to Philip Pearson, who lived near, to ascertain the chance of procuring meat and bread for the men, and food for the horses; and if these necessary articles could be had, to provide for their transportation to the destitute camp. For one week Washington's men and horses were abundantly furnished from Mr. Pearson's farm. And he too, like his friend Harrison, waived all compensation present or prospective.

THE TORIES.—A word may be said in apology for the Tories. In the darkest period of the war, President Rutledge, whose genius could alone cast a gleam of hope across the gloom that rested upon the country, established his headquarters at Orangeburgh, by proclamation convened all his militias, and in language which few could mistake and none resist, he invited the Tories to a consultation. The Tories came in by companies, by battalions and regiments, and were formed into a Brigade by the name of State Troops, under Henderson, and did admirable service at the great battle of the Entaw.

An anecdote connected with the aforesaid proclamation deserves to be recorded. Rutledge had prepared his proclamation "in thoughts that breathe and in words that burn," and called upon his ready writers to copy it off for circulation in the most finished style of chirography. A friend in his confidence suggested the great advantages of sending it forth in print. The President admitted it; but added, the British are in possession of the only press in the State, and to obtain even the temporary use of it is impossible. "That difficulty,'" responded the gentlemen, "may be overcome; there is a gunsmith living a few miles off who never failed in a solitary attempt to accomplish anything he put his hand to." "Well, please to send for him." In a short time Mr. Mucklerath, the gun-smith, reported himself to the President, and respectfully inquired his commands. "My wishes," said the President, "are that you cast forthwith a set of types to print my proclamation. Can you do it?" Mucklerath pleaded ignorance of the art of type founding, but said he would try. Pewter plates and all procurable materials for the important job were immediately put in requisition. The ingenious mechanic went to work; some went to manufacturing printer's ink; suitable paper was procured, the types were finished in a day, the printers went to work, and on the following day out came the Proclamation in admirable style.

JOHN HAMPTON was a Virginian by birth, and emigrated with his father's family to Carolina in early life,—anterior to 1770. Old Mr. Hampton settled in the mountain region, not being willing to trust his health to the middle or low country. A few years afterwards, he and several of his family fell victims to the bloody Cherokees. On the breaking out of the Revolutionary War, John Hampton espoused the Whig cause with zeal, and continued in the service until the battle of the Entaws, where in command of a battalion of State troops, he closed his military career. On the return of peace, he married and settled a few years in the District of Beaufort. He ultimately made his permanent home on the banks of Broad river, Lexington District. Here he resided till the day of his death, scrupulously discharging the duties of life like an honest man and a good citizen.

Major Hampton's education was respectable, which as long as he lived he continued to add to and improve. He wrote well, he composed with facility and marked correctness. His conversation was light, beautiful, instructive. Wit was the distinguishing characteristic of his mind, and his flashes of merriment are not yet forgotten by his old friends. The Major was of middle size, symmetrically proportioned, and of extraordinary beauty. He was frequently returned a member of the Lower House for Lexington, and served several terms as Senator for Lexington and Newberry. His wit was dreaded by the verdant, and opinions respected by all classes. He died at his seat about 1807.

JOHN BUCHANAN, of Fairfield District, was a native of the North of Ireland, and arrived in this country before the commencement of hostilities,—was made a Captain in the regular army. He was with his company in Williamson's campaign against the Cherokees in 1776. Every morning at daybreak the sage commander ordered the swivels to be fired off so that the Cherokees knew more about him that he did about himself, and picked their time and place to annoy him. Williamson afterwards went off with British. He was a Scotchman, and did not know a letter in the book. In that campaign, in a trifling skirmish, fell young Salvadore, a youth of extraordinary endowments and of rare promise.

Capt. Buchanan was afterwards at the seige of Savannah and fall of Charleston. The days of his soldiering having drawn to a close, he returned to Fairfield where he had numerous friends and relations,—married, purchased a farm on Little River, engaged in the ruinous experiment of mill-building on that impetuous stream; afterwards engaged in the business of Inn-holder, in Winnsborough, which he found profitable. He was rewarded with the office of Judge of Ordinary, which brought him in a snug salary, and which, together with the profits of a small farm, enabled him to retire from the Inn, and placed him in easy circumstances.

Such was the neatness and regularity with which his office of Ordinary was kept, that it was indeed a pattern office. The latter part of his life was devoted to religious duties, and his conduct, in all its relations, strikingly exemplary. Capt. Buchanan was tall, and of considerable personal dignity; his manners were those of a perfect gentleman,—but he never could lay aside the stateliness of a veteran officer. He died about 1831.

MAJOR HENRY MOORE, a native of Ireland, a fine mathematician, many years a teacher,—a Capt.—Lieut. in Reg't of S. C. Artillery in 1776,—in fight at Beaufort Island, and siege of Charleston, afterwards sheriff of Fairfield, and died at his beautiful seat near Winnsborough in 1845.

GEN. JOHN PEARSON, eldest son of John P. (who was native of Berkshire, England, and early settled in Carolina) was born in what is now Richland Co., S. C., in 1743. Under the instruction of his father, and with a little school education, he became a very good English scholar. He was, however, cut out for action, and devoted very little time to the cultivation of letters. He was attentive to the main chance,—acquired considerable money, purchased a few hands and a noble plantation on Broad river, in Fairfield, where he fixed himself for life. At the commencement of the war, Mr. Pearson was appointed Major of Volunteers (every Whig was a volunteer), and took the field under Sumter. He did much service under the command of the *Game Cock* of the Revolution, and was sometimes dispatched on distant and perilous duty. He knew what it was to thirst, starve, to sleep on the cold damp ground in pestilent swamps, and go in rags and tatters through the bitterness of winter. Major Pearson finished his military career with a high character for courage, activity, and conduct; and no officer of his grade carried with him to the walks of private life a higher and more affectionate regard of those he had commanded in days of peril and difficulty.

The Fairfield people sent him perhaps oftener than for one term to the Legislature when that body met at Charleston. On the reorganization of the militia system in 1796, there was a vacancy for a Colonel's command in the newly constructed Fairfield regiment, and he was elected over Major Turner; and subsequently attained the rank of Brigadier-General. In 1804, he was elected State Senator for the District of Fairfield, Richland and Chester; and at the expiration of his senatorial term, he dropt all public employment, devoting the balance of his days to neighborly duties and the improvement of his estate. All through life he was the blessed peace-maker and the adjuster of difficulties. He reconciled, as with authority, husbands and wives who had become discontented and dissatisfied parents and children. No one who ever came to his Chancery ever left it displeased, and all said, or thought or felt, "blessed is the peacemaker." He accumulated a large estate, exercised unlimited hospitality, and practiced a liberal charity. He died about 1820, in the 78th year of his age. The love of his country was the last glow that warmed his old heart.

GEN. RICHARD WINN was from the Old Dominion. He immigrated to Carolina a considerable time before the war, and served as a clerk in a counting-house on Charleston for some years. He then took a position in the Virginia colony in Fairfield. Here he followed the business of a land surveyor until just before the coast was whitened with the canvass of the British ships, and lit up with red coats. He received the appointment of First Lieutenant in Capt. Woodward's company of Rangers, and served on Sullivan's Island when Sir Peter Parker made his formidable attack on the palmetto fort.

He received advices that the Tories and Indians, backed by a few British troops, were committing sad havoc in the most southern part of Georgia. The country was totally defenceless. Fort St. Illa and Fort Barrington had been both abandoned. It was desirable that the former should be placed in repair and thoroughly garrisoned with a view to hold the enemy in check, and restrain his depredations. The General promised the command in this important service to any officer of the rank of Captain who could raise eighty volunteers for the purpose. Winn was now Captain, but he was not the first to beat up for volunteers; several captains attempted to do so, and failed. Capt. Winn at length raised his flag, and ordered out his music. In less than 25 minutes his number was made up. He made no unnecessary delay; he and his men were speedily equipped and mounted, and they took up the line of march for their distant point of destination.

On approaching Fort St. Illa, a considerable body of the enemy were discovered. He divided his force into two equal parts; one he left to find its way to the fort, and to preserve military stores committed to its charge. The other he put himself at the head of, and ordered a charge upon the enemy. He declined returning the Whig fire, and set off with speed for his flotilla in the river eleven miles below. Winn killed 14 of them on the chase, wounded as many more, and recovered all the property which they had gathered in their plundering excursion into the country, with a quantity of arms and ammunition. He returned to his friends well rewarded for his long race, and the slight peril incident to his enterprise.

Capt. Winn found the fort in an utterly ruined condition, and set about constructing a new one much larger than the old one. He took the axe and the spade himself, and there were no lookers-on in camp. A strong block-house, inclosed with huge palisades, soon sprang up sufficient to afford protection against any number of small arms. The fort was scarcely completed when a large body of Tories and Indians, sustained by a few regular troops, made their approach. A flag was sent in to demand the instantaneous surrender of the fort. The Captain knew the strength of his position, and the character of the brave men under his command. He declined the surrender, demanded, and prepared for his defence, as it was evident, against fearful odds. The firing commenced on both sides, and was kept up almost incessantly for near three days. Many of the enemy climbed up into the neighboring trees with a view to fire over the pickets into the body of the fort; but the block-house rendered their efforts unavailing, and many a one never descended alive from their high nest in the tree-tops.

On the evening of the third day of the fight, Gen. Prevost came up from Augusta with three pieces of cannon and a strong regular force. A flag demanding an unconditional surrender arrived speedily at the fort. Winn now saw his case was hopeless, as he had no power to resist artillery. He therefore determined to surrender, but insisted on certain terms to be settled by articles of capitulation. The Commissioners were appointed to draw up the terms, to which Maj. Gen. Prevost and Capt. Winn set their hands,—they were very liberal and favorable to the Americans. The gates of the fort were then thrown open, and many of Prevost's officers entered. It is said, that when he saw a Captain and a few ragged militia who inflicted on his motley army damage to an unprecedented amount, he groaned in spirit.

On first arriving at the fort, the Americans had turned their horses into the range, many straggled off, and not a few fell into the hands of the enemy. Three-fourths of the men had to march on foot to their distant homes in middle and upper Carolina. As the force under Capt. Winn at Fort Illa were three-fifths of them soldiers in his company of Rangers, the surrender operated as a dissolution of the company.

As soon as he was exchanged, he was appointed Colonel of the Fairfield Whig Regiment, marched at its head, and joined Gen. Sumter. Except when detailed on special duty, which was the case often, and in which he always acted effectually, and heroically, he was always by his General's side, and participated in his principal battles. He was with him among many other trying occasions at the battle of Hanging Rock, where he received a wound through the body which was near proving fatal. In that battle no man quailed,—every American behaved like a veteran. Cornwallis was heard to say that no battle fell heavier on the British, considering the numbers engaged, the battle of Bunker Hill excepted. Recovering slowly from his dreadful wound, the Colonel returned again to his command, and was always at his post of duty. He never returned to the delights of home, or the business of civil life as long as there was a Briton in the land, or a Tory persisting in his rebellion.

On the return of peace he visited his friends, and resumed his long abandoned labors. He shortly afterwards married, settled a farm, purchased negroes and stock, and went to work to provide for his family. In 1788, he was appointed United States Superintendent of Indian Affairs for the Creek (Southern Indians) Nation. He was called several times to serve in the Legislature, and presided in the County Court while that system was allowed to continue. On the reorganization of the militia in 1796, he was elected a Brigadier-General, and some years after Major-General of the Upper Division. About 1793 he beat Gen. Sumter for Congress, but was beaten in turn by Sumter at the ensuing election. About 1796, (1801—L. C. D.) Sumter was elected to the U. S. Senate, and Winn succeeded him as Representative, and held that high appointment by many successive elections, down to 1812. He was twice very fully opposed, and at every other was chosen without opposition. He belonged to the Jefferson party in politics, and never during the whole course of his public life was he suspected of a change in sentiment. Gen. Winn was a highly respectable member, but no speaker. One efficient speech, however, he made about the time of the declaration of the War of 1812. The bill looking to the war, providing for an increase of the army, made provision for calling into the field a great many volunteer regiments. A federal member ridiculed the idea of opposing British veterans with raw volunteers. Winn was stung by his remark, and addressing the Speaker replied to him, that "he had commanded volunteers, and had seen how that description of troops could fight. He had seen them meet British veterans who considerably outnumbered them, and had seen them beat British veterans in the open field. I will give that gentleman a picked regiment of his favorite veterans, and I will put myself in command of a regiment of volunteers, we will have a meeting, and if I don't flog him (popping his hands emphatically) *my head for it!*" The Federal member evidently displayed signs of discomfiture, and the Republicans openly congratulated Winn for his triumph.

Gen. Winn had the usual weakness of putting his hand to paper as security, and as is usual generally had the money to pay. Between 1795 and 1810, he paid security debts to the amount of $50,000. In his long absences from home, his overseers did what was good in their own eyes—that is, never to consult the good of the employer. His plantation was unproductive of profits, and his circumstances were not prosperous. He sold his lands at good advantage, removed with an aching heart from his ancient seat, and a country he loved, to a body of lands he owned on Duck River (Tennessee). Here, after some years, in the depths of the solitude, and amidst strangers, he breathed his last at a good old age. Gen. Winn was upwards of six feet in height, and indefinitely well formed. His countenance was noble and majestic, and beamed with the warmth of benevolence and kindness. His port was noble, and his manners dignified and elegant.

THOS. WOODWARD rmoved with a large family from Virginia, and settled in Fairfield, S. C., about 1765. Took an active part in the Regulation in putting down the Scofilites; in 1775, app'd a Captain in Col. Wm. Thomson's regiment of Rangers, and aided in the defence of Charleston in 1776, with his regiment. As Capt. W. was now near sixty years of age, he resigned and returned to his home,—where he aided efficiently in keeping the Tories in check. He was a terror to evil-doers, and the dry bones of the Tories shook at the very name of Woodward. About eight years after peace he lost his life in heading a party in attacking and breaking up a gang of thieves. He was considerably over common size, possessing strong but agreeable features, and his form was symmetry itself. (He was ever regarded as one of the heroic men of Fairfield. L. C. D.)

ENTAW BATTLE.—STATE TROOPS.—The able and distinguished Gen. Henderson was placed in chief command of the mounted State troops, and history has done them nothing but justice in ascribing to them the highest praise. That part of them who acted on horse-back performed their part to admiration. They charged upon the enemy, poured in their dreadful rifle shots, or pistol shots as the case required, with the alacrity and coolness of veterans.

Fairfields' population during the Revolution was about equally divided between the Whigs and Tories. Among the former· is enumerated Adjutant James Thurston, Benjamin May, Isham and Daniel Dansby and Reuben Harrison.

COL. JOHN CHRISTIAN SENF was a native of Saxony, landed at New York as an engineer in the Hessian troops, having the rank of Captain. In his own country he had heard every evil spoken of the Americans and their cause. But Senf was of a noble nature, and he was determined to judge for himself. He read the State papers, and such pamphlets as had been written by American patriots in vindication of the American Revolution, and he came to the conclusion that the Colonies had right and justice on their side. When his mind was fairly made up he tendered his sword to his commander and candidly stated his reasons, declaring that he never would serve a day against so honorable and magnanimous people. He was immediately placed under guard, but escaped to the American camp. Washington was no stranger to Senf's history and character, and gave him a cordial reception, and gave him immediate appointment in the engineer service. Senf served with the entire approbation of the Commander-in-chief to the end of the War. The Baron Van Binkel was the Dutch Minister to the United States during and for some time after the Revolutionary contest; he brought with him to Philadelphia a daughter, not handsome, but very learned and accomplished. Capt. Senf became acquainted with her, and obtained her ready assent to marry him. The Baron grew boisterous when Capt. Senf asked his consent to the nuptials; he raved his dissent in the true style of a roused and exasperated Dutchman. He never would be reconciled to his son-in-law, but despised him with a fiendish constancy. Before he left Philadelphia, he purchased stock in the Bank of the U. S. amounting to $40,000, which he transferred to Madame Senf on certain terms and conditions, by which she was entitled to draw the dividends while Senf lived, and after his death, if she survived him, the capital.

SANTEE CANAL.—A Company at an early period after the war obtained a liberal charter for opening the navigation of the Catawba river from Camden Ferry to the North Carolina line. The company engaged the services of Senf to superintend, etc. He brought his family on to Carolina, and settled at Rocky Mount, waiting the orders of the company. They had promised him a complete salary should they go on with the worn, which they assured him they would do, but never did. Senf did not obtain during the long years he resided at the Mount a single dollar. The Governor conferred upon Senf the empty title of Civil and Military Engineer of South Carolina, with the rank of Lieutenant-Colonel. It was an unsalaried office.

MAJ. W. SYLES, of Syles' Ford P. C. June 20, 1858, gives a brief account of the Syles family and of the early habits and customs of pioneer times,—and says: The Syles were originally from Virginia,—first to Bute Co., N. C., and then to S. C. Refers to Pearson's history, which, he adds, "I will send in a few days," and wishes the Pearson Narrative returned.

"Of all the name, however, Col. James Syles, a brother of cousin of my grandfather (Anomanos Syles,—a Captain in the Rev'n and a Colonel after,—in Jas. Williams' reg't) was the most active. He was in constant service as a Colonel during the most, if not the whole, of the war. In company with Col. Lacey, of Chester, he commanded, the center of the battle of Hanging Rock, in Lancaster."

ENTAW BATTLE.—Conversations with Judge O'Neall:

"Dick Johnson, of Edgefield, lived near Hamburg. He was a remarkable man. He was under Col. LeRoy Hammond (Samuel, L. C. D.) at the Entaw; he charged upon the brick house, jumped off of his horse, and taking a nail from his pocket stuck it into the touch-hole of a cannon, and driving it home with his basket-hilted sword, said: "You have plagued us all day; you shall plague us no more." He went into that battle with a pair of white pants and white vest, and came out as bloody as a butcher from head to foot.

Robert Stark was at Entaw; the father of Judge O'Neall saw him while Adjutant of LeRoy Hammond's regiment, muster his men with his coat sleeves torn off to his elbows.

Robert Starke's father (continued Judge O'Neall) lived at the Ridge in Edgefield. It was his daughter who informed Cruger at Ninety Six, of Lord Rawdon's approach. She rode down the lane with a letter in her hand, and when near the gate, held up the letter, and putting spurs to her horse was admitted safely into the fort. She had married a British officer named Willison.

Rob't. Starke was a huge man, though not tall, with the voice of a lion. When admitted to the bar he was unpromising. Old P. Carnes said on one occasion: "May it please your honor, I don't think the young man knows what an assault and battery is." "I don't?" said Starke rising, and shaking his fist in his face, said: "That is assault, and that" (hitting him over the eye) "is battery." Carnes said: "I didn't think he had that much sense." Starke was speaker of the House, and solicitor many years.

HAYES' STATION MASSACRE.—Wm. Dunlap was spared, and on being asked about it years after, said: "Good God, sir, I have not thought of that since: I was put down in the ring, and the man on my right, and the one on my left, were cut to pieces, and I knew no more till I was discharged the next day at Young's Mill, now Ogle's Mills, on Beaver Dam Creek."

COL. JAMES MAYSON was a scotchman,—left the Rangers, and took protection.

JOHN PURVIS was aid to Williamson.

FROM G. W. MEANS, GLENN'S SPRING, AUG. 28, 1858.

SAMUEL CLOWNEY was a native of Ireland, first settled on Catawba river in North Carolina. He left his native isle in company with but one male friend. After the war of the Revolution he married and settled in Union District, 8 m. N. W. of the C. H. where he remained up to the time of his death, Sept. 27, 1824, in the 82nd year of his age.

The Home Journal, I understand, gives the particulars with regard to the capture of five Tories by Samuel Clowney during the Revolution. Substantially it is as follows: A few days previous to the fight between the Tories and Liberty Men or Whigs at Cedar Springs, Clowney and a few others had obtained leave of absence from the commanding officer at Cedar Springs, for the purpose of visiting their homes. They lived on Fairforest creek, in a settlement known as Ireland, on account of the large number of settlers from the Emerald Isle,—all of whom were staunch Whigs. On their way home, the party left with a Mrs. Foster some clothes to be washed, and appointed a particular hour and place where they should meet her and get them on their return to the camp. In accordance with that appointment with Mrs. Foster (who took a lively interest and rendered efficient aid in the Revolutionary cause), when the party reached Kelso's Creek, about 5 miles from Cedar Springs, they diverged from the road through the woods to the appointed place, leaving Clowney and a negro man named Paul to hold their horses until they should return with the washing. In the meantime five armed Tories in making their way to a Tory camp in the neighborhood, passed Clowney and Paul with the horses. The Tories came right up on them before they knew they were there; and to their utter astonishment they received from Clowny peremptory orders to surrender. Being somewhat slow in surrendering, the command was repeated, and the consequences of disobeying orders brought to view, when they surrendered. Paul carried their guns, and they were at once marched across the creek to the place where the rest of the party were in company with Mrs. Foster.

L. MILES, to Dr. Logan, Spartanburg, Aug. 11, 1858; says he was born Feb. 1, 1782,—born and raised within 3 miles of Blackstock's, and still lives there. I went to see Old Blackstock's when I was a boy. He was an old Irishman when the British and Tories camped at his home or nearby, he used to pilot them to my father's to rob and plunder.

I have heard my mother say all the way she could keep anything to eat was, to put it in a gum in the jam of the house, and cover it with ashes, and they would pass it for an ash gum. The Tories would strip beds and take everything they or their horses could use at their camps.

BLACKSTOCK'S BATTLE.—I have heard Golding Finsley talk a great deal about the war. He was at the battle of Blackstock's, when Major Money, a British officer, was riding in front on a white horse. Some one of Finsley's commanders said to him: "Can't you throw that fellow?" Finsley replied: "I can try." He took aim at him, and he fell to rise no more.

MUSGROVE'S MILLS BATTLE.—Finsley was also in this fight. He said they killed many British and Tories as they fled across the stream, and shot them while in the act of crossing. After they had got over, one fellow squatted down, turned his buttocks and stopped in derision at the Americans. Finsley's commander said to him: "Can't you turn that fellow over?" Finsley replied: "I can try." Finsley had a good rifle, sat down, took good aim, shot, and turned him over. They took him up and carried him off.

Finsley was at the Cowpens. He was a valiant soldier. He has been dead some 5 or 6 years.

MAJ. S. T. SIM'S TRADITIONS OF UNION DIST.

(No date.)

LIEUT. COL. CHARLES SIMS.

Long before the Revolution, the Sims' family came from England,—among the first settlers and settled in Virginia. Charles Sims, the son of Matthew, came directly from Albemarle Co., Va., to S. C. in the fall of 1777. His wife's name was Isabella Bowles,—mentioned in Mrs. Ellet's *Women of the Revolution*. He brought with him four daughters and a son Wm. (father of Maj. S. T. Sims and Knight Sims.) One of the daughters then married, Mrs. McDaniel. Mr. Sims settled at the mouth of Tinker's Creek on the Tiger. He soon entered with his whole soul into the partisan service of the War, under Brandon and Waters. He was of good education, and a good surveyor,—was inspector of tobacco in Charleston,—and a faithful magistrate after the war, and died at 85 in 1816. He was of great activity and strength to the last, and would drive deer with the young men from 80 to 85. He lived in great temperance. Is buried in the family burial ground on Broad river.

At the fall of Augusta or siege of Savannah, he was sent by Gen. Pickens with a hundred men to guard a pass on Steven's Creek, in Edgefield. The weather was hot, and the place sickly (in May or June, 1781, doubtless, when Pickens and Lee took Augusta,—for the siege of Savannah was in Sept. or Oct., 1779;) his men were all with himself soon down with the fever. He was afterwards disposed to charge Gen.

Pickens with a want of due regard to the welfare of his men. Being relieved he made his way home, and was just recovering his health, when (being at home on account of his sickness) a Tory scout surrounded the house and took him prisoner. This was probably Bill Lee, who operated largely in this neighborhood. Cornwallis was then at Spring Hill, Lexington District, on Congaree Creek. A drum-head court having been called, he and young Johnson (see Dr. Sam Otterson, Shelby) were condemned to die. Johnson was brother-in-law to old Maj. Sam Otterson. He was hung on a tree near his own house. On Congaree Creek, near Cornwallis, in a Tory camp, Sims was already tied up to the limb of a tree that was still standing on the old road that crossed the creek at that time, just to be turned off,—the cap had been drawn over his eyes, when an officer riding up from Cornwallis' camp, asked who that was, and on being told it was Charles Sims, he ordered him instantly to be taken down. He recognized him as an old schoolmate. This officer's name was Maj. George. They had been schoolmates in Virginia. George took him to Cornwallis, and procured for him not only a pardon, but a parole.

He returned home, but was obliged to lie concealed in the woods to escape the vengeance of the Tories. He had been instrument in the condemnation and execution of a notorious Tory of the Fairforest region. It was on this occasion that he was taken in, out of the woods, and protected by a good Quaker, old Eli Cook, who lived near the old Quaker church on Tinker Creek,—a kind and humane man. Sims had been for some time fed in the woods by his wife. Cook knew also his hiding place, and a deep snow having fallen, he was fearful that Sims would freeze,—went and brought him in, and concealed him in his hay loft, which stood near his house. He had his arms with him. One bright moon-light night, a Tory scout rode into the old Quaker's yard, and demanded of him where Sims was concealed. Sims heard every word that was spoken; he believed his time had come, thinking that the old Quaker had betrayed him. But he was quickly reassured. Cook managed the difficulty with admirable skill. "Ah I not a King's man? Have you any right to think I would conceal a rebel? Am I Sims' keeper?" These evasive inquiries were made so rapidly and earnestly that the Tories were completely deceived, and searched no farther for their victim. Sims all the time lay in a few feet of them, his gun and pistol cocked, prepared to sell his life dearly, if the Quaker had proved traitor.

It was about this time that Bill Lee, a leading officer of Cunningham's Bloody Scout, made a famous onslaught on the Whig settlers of Tiger and Tinker Creek. He came among the first to the house of Mrs. Sims,—the Major was an outlaw in the woods. Mrs. Sims having come out, he ordered her to prepare to leave the premises; he wished to put in her house one of the King's men. Besides her two children she had with her her daughter, Mrs. McDaniels. "How can you require this of me, sir? You have driven off my husband; you have taken my horses and negroes." "That is not my look-out, Madam; I will give you a week to move; if at the end of that time I find you here, I'll lock you up in the house and burn you in it."

An old man named Freelove Gregory, a non-combatant, hearing of her situation, came down with some slides and moved her and her effects some 15 miles away on Brown's Creek to a place now owned by David Gondelock. She afterwards got with her children under the protection of Dr. Joseph Alexander, of York. He kept a sort of hospital, where he inoculatd the Whig families who were exposed to the small-pox. Lee and his party now plundered the house, and while in the act, Mrs. Sims remembered that the McFunkins and Jollys, who lived some six miles higher up the creek, had just come in from their hiding places to see their families; she knew that not a man of them would escape the merciless swords of the Tories, if they were caught. She called her son, Wm. Sims, then a lad of twelve years, to her, and whispered: "My son, the McFunkins and Jollys are all at home, and will be taken by Lee, if not apprised in time of their danger. Can't you very soon run there by the path a nearer way than the main road, and tell them of their danger?" William at once consented to go, though it was already nearly dark, and the way a wilderness full of wolves and other beasts of prey. He set out at once in a full run. He said the wolves soon began to howl around him, but grasping an old jack-knife he had in his pocket, he felt quite safe. When he arrived at McFunkins, the family had just sat down to supper. Their arms were lying by them, and their horses saddled in the stables, ready for a surprise. He rushed in out of breath, and exclaimed: "Ma, the Tories are coming." They were soon in the saddle and running for shelter, but had hardly disappeared on one side of the house before Lee and his scout came in at the other. Young Sims had hurried on to tell the Jollys of the impending danger. They all escaped, and doubtless owed their lives to the intrepidity of young William Sims, for the Tories thirsted for their blood.

As soon as William Sims had set out for the McFunkins, Mrs. Sims continued to reproach and remonstrate with Lee for his villainy, in order to detain them as long as possible from the attack on her friends higher up the creek. While this was going on, B. Musgrove, one of Lee's men, went up to the bed on which Mrs. McDaniel's children were sleeping, and took from it one of the two blankets. As that covered them, it was an exceedingly cold evening and raining. As Musgrove went out of the door with the blanket, Mrs. Mc Daniel said to him: "Beaks Musgrove, you will answer for that at the day of judgment." "By D—d, Madame," he replied, "if I am to have that long credit, I'll take the other." And returning to the bed took that also.

After Wm. Sims' effort to save the McFunkins and Jollys, he became so obnoxious to the Tories that it became necessary for his friends to conceal him the best way they could, and he actually lived for a long time in the family of the good Quaker, Eli Cook, dressed as a female, and passing as a little girl.

Whatever was the date of Capt. Sims' retreat into Virginia, he had returned, and was in active service again as Capt. in So.

Carolina, in June, 1780, according to the papers in the Sec. Office. (This surely was long before he went to Va., for there was no Tory warfare in Union and Spartanburg till after the fall of Charleston, May, 1780.—L. C. D.)

Capt. Charles Sims in his private character, was a most estimable man,—not only a true and enlightened patriot, but a steady, conscientious, law-abiding citizen.

After his return from Virginia, he served 560 days.

COL. WM. HENDERSON was also a distinguished officer of the Revolution. He came from N. C., from Roanoke, near the Virginia line, and settled a single man, on the Pacolet, on a place now owned by Sam'l. Hanes, adjoining the plantation of Major Star Sims. He lived there with his sister, Mrs. John Beckham. After the war he married on the High Hills of Santee, a Mrs. Hunter (?), and lived here the remainder of his days. He commanded the State troops at the Battle of Entaw *Springs. He was a Colonel under Sumter; but Sumter, from some cause, not taking part in this battle, Henderson took command, and led one of the most famous charges in the war. He was a tall fine looking man, with black eyes. He left but one child, Eliza, who afterwards married Simon Taylor, nephew of old Col. Thomas Taylor, of Columbia. She removed to Alabama (Louisiana), where she became a widow. Henderson seems to have been a man of estimable private character. His memory is revered by his family.

John Beckham, his father-in-law, was a most active Whig, and fearless scout. While Morgan was encamped on Grindal's Shoals, he kept him in constant motion, and he did valuable service. On one occasion, when closely pressed by the Light Horse of Tarleton, he plunged headlong down a fearful bank into the river, and made his escape. The spot is still well known, and often pointed out. It was on the plantation of old Wm. Hodge, who was also a true Whig. A comrade named Easterwood, from whom the shoals take their name, was with him in this race. Easterwood rode a big clumsy horse, and was big and heavy himself. His horse striking his foot against a log, fell sprawling, and Easterwood was made prisoner. Beckhams mare a magnificent animal, soon left them in the rear. He could have got off easier, but stopping at Hodge's to light his pipe, (he was an incessant smoker), the British were close upon him, while he was yet holding the fire. He swore he would light it before he budged a foot. After gaining the opposite side of Pacolet, he slapped his thigh, and looking back at his pursuers, "Shoot and be d____d," he cried, his pipe still in his mouth. He is said to have done all his scouting and fighting with his pipe in his mouth. He survived the war, and lies buried on Hodge's plantation. His only son removed to Kentucky; his daughters all married and moved to the West.

WM. HODGE was also a good Whig. His place was some three miles above Grindal's Shoals; it is now occupied by his grandson, Moses Hodge. While Morgan was encamped at the Shoals, his house was plundered and burnt by Tarleton's men, the old man made prisoner, and sent to Camden jail. He, however, escaped and returned home.

JAMES MOSELEY, another Whig of the Pacolet, lived some two miles from the shoals on Sandy Run. His place is now in possession of Shelton McWhorter. He was a famous hunter and woodsman; his trade, that of a blacksmith. He came originally from Virginia, and settled first on the headwaters of the Yadkin, at the foot of the Yellow Mountain. He was then 14 years old. Here he was associated for a time with the celebrated Daniel Boone, and was preparing to join him in his expedition to Kentucky, when he was prevented by his father, on the plea of youth. He did much valuable service as a scout,—always on foot.

He was once sent from the High Hills by Sumter to Col. Tom. Taylor, of Columbia, with a valuable express. Taylor's cabin stood on the high hill that (since) overlooked the waterworks and much of the valley of the Broad river. He says Taylor was sitting at a table when he walked in, his sword by his side.

A post oak, known as Moseley's Tree, is still standing immediately on the road to the Grindal Shoals ford, just below the house of Garland Meng. Everybody knows it in that country, and no sacrilegious hand would dare touch it. Mosely was out hunting and having taken a small deer, was returning home with it on his shoulders. The wolves getting a scent of the blood, were soon on his trail; he heard them coming, and knew that he must make an effort to save both himself and meat. The latter he sunk in a neighboring branch, and having climbed up into the post oak, waited their coming. They bayed him all night. "Why did you not shoot them, Mr. Moseley?" was asked him afterwards, "You had your rifle." "Because," he said, "I wanted to kill the leader of the troop, and it was too dark to distinguish him; as soon as light began to appear, they began to enlarge the circle they were constantly making around the tree." He then singled him out, and shot him. The rest retreated to their dens.

DANIEL MCFUNKIN, brother of Major McFunkin, was with Col. Brandon at his defeat on Fairforest. In the rout, he was overtaken by a British officer, who ran his thrust sword through his body. The blade entered between his shoulders, and came out in the breast, and came so far through that McFunkin caught it and held it tight in his agony. The officer said to him: "My good fellow, if you will let go, I will draw it out, and give you as little pain as possible." He did so and the officer putting his foot against McFunkin's shoulder, as he sat on his horse, extracted the sword, upon which McFunkin fell to the ground. Mrs. C. Sims attended him for this wound, and under her skilful treatment, he recovered, and lived to a very old man,—if he is not yet dead. Wm. Sims, who went with his mother to see McFunkin, used to say he made the most awful groans while suffering from his wound, he ever heard mortal man utter. He moved to Pendleton.

Old Maj. S. Otterson was in Brandon'd defeat, as well as Blackstock's.

COL. JOSEPH HUGHES.—See R. W. Hughes, of New York, about his father, Col. Jos. Hughes. His grandfather was murdered by the Tories while in search of his hogs. His body was pierced by seven wounds. He lived on the road leading from Unionville to Chesterville, at McCool's Ferry on Broad River. It is now Caife's Ferry. Joseph after looking at the mangled corpse of his father, raised his gun, and swore he would kill every Tory he met. He was a famous rifleman; he trained himself to fire the rifle as quick as a duellist would a pistol. He was in person almost a giant, and of great activity as well as strength. In daring he was utterly reckless,—knew not what fear was. He performed a desperate feat in Chester, in an attack on a body of Tories in a log house in an open field. The siege was about to be given up, when Hughes with great indignation, swore he would never leave a Tory in that house. He then kindled a torch, and approaching the house under cover of another as near as he could, he suddenly darted out to run the remainder of the distance exposed to the rifles of a platoon who guarded an opening extending the whole length of the house. The whole line fired as he darted out, but just at that instant, knowing what they would do, he stooped low, and every ball passed clear over his head. In the next instant he was under the building blowing up his fire. The Tories saw the game was up, and surrendered. The father of Dr. Winsmith was present in this skirmish.

Hughes was as famous for his independence and moral courage as for his physical hardihood. Some time after the war, a case was pending in Chester Court in which it became necessary to ascertain whether a certain notorious marauding Tory by the name of M____e was dead or alive; and if dead, at what time he died. It being supposed that Hughes knew something of him he was examined on commission, when he fearlessly acknowledged that he had shot the said M..e since the war as one of the miscreants against whom he had sworn eternal vengeance.

He later in life removed with his family, and son-in-law, Jack Mabry, to the western edge of Alabama. When passing through the Indian nation he came across an old refugee Tory named Radcliff, living in the midst of the Indians and negroes. Hughes eyed him very closely for sometime, and suddenly exclaimed in the gruff blountness peculiar to him: "I know you, sir. You are a scamp of a Tory (the old man had become a Presbyterian then, and did not swear); I ran you, sir, from Chester District and nothing but an accident saved your life. I am a good mind to make way with you now. Hop about now, or I'll do it yet." Mabry was alarmed; a large company of half-breed Indians and negroes devoted to the old refugee's interest were standing around, and Radcliff himself, was no mean looking antagonist. But he was thoroughly cowed, and was annoyingly obsequious as long as they remained with him. Mabry says he could not sleep that night; but the Colonel threw himself down, and was soon snoring as if nothing had happened. Before he spoke to Radcliff on this occasion, he looked at him with a furtive glance, as if painful recollections had been aroused, and when he said: "I know you," Radcliff replied, "No, I guess not, sir. Don't know you." "Don't you know me? Have you forgotten when I ran you from Broad river?"

His neighbors said of him, that he was destitute of all sense of fear. He was an elder in Bullock's Creek church. He died in Alabama of a cancer, but was very aged. To the last he could bring down a buck in the wilds of his adopted State. It was said of Hughes that the worst thing he ever did was taking a fair shot with his rifle at a woman, whose name was White. She belonged to the Tories, and had done much mischief in informing them of the hiding places of the Whigs. The ball struck a sapling, and glanced from the intended victim.

At the battle of Cowpens, having got separated from his troops, he was attacked by a couple of British dragoons; he seized a small sapling, and with this defended his head from the strokes of one, and with his rifle warded off the blows of the other. One of the Savages, a comrade from his neighborhood, seeing his situation, ran to his assistance, and having shot one of the Dragoons, Hughes clubbed his rifle and soon dispatched the other.

Enquire of R. W. Hughes of the incident of his father, Sharp and others taking some 200 Tories on the waters of Brown's Creek, of Union; and of Hughes burning out the Tories (as already related) at the risk of his life.

REV. JAMES H. SAYE'S NOTES.—SEPT. 23rd, 1858.

COL. THOS. BRANDON.—Says Maj. J. Young: Col. Thos. Brandon was a native of Pennsylvania. He came to this country when quite a young man, a good many years before the war of the Revolution. He married, before the war, Elizabeth McCool, who owned the Ferry now owned by Scaife. He entered the service as a Captain in the Spartan regiment in 1775. He became Colonel of the 2nd Spartan regiment when formed some time bfore the fall of Charleston. At the head of this he continued till the close of the war, and with it, or a part of it, he was in most of the battles. He was at Musgrove's, King's Mountain, Cowpens, and many small affairs. After the war he as a Brigadier General, member of the Legislature, etc.

Col. Farr was in many battles, and seems to have succeeded Steen as Lieut. Col. of the 2nd Spartan regiment.

Lieut. Col. James Steen was in a number of battles, and seems to have been a gallant officer. Major Joesph McFunkin survived nearly all of his comrades in this region, and remembered more details of service than any man with whom I ever conversed. You will find his narrative in the January number of the Magnolia, 1843, by Judge O'Neall. Some things are in that which were put in by the Judge. It needs a careful revision, as well as the one published by myself at a subsequent period. He was in the "Snow campaign" in 1775; with Williamson in the Indian expedition, 1776; in various tours of duty before the fall of Charleston. Was at Rocky Mount, Hanging Rock, Musgrove's Mill, Blackstock's, and the Cowpens. Was wounded in the right arm in March, 1781,—arm broke.

Had the smallpox and was taken prisoner and kept till June. After that was in no battle.

Joseph Jolly was a Captain in 1776. John Jolly was a Lieutenant in 1780, and was killed in that or the following year.

Benjamin Jolly is mentioned as a Major by several men after the battle of Cowpens. He probably succeeded Maj. McFunkin, as he seems to have been quite active after March, 1781. He was at the battle of Entaw, and commanded the men from Union at that place. He was a man of fine appearance and of great muscular power. He was in most of the battles in 1780.

Joseph Hughes is not mentioned much before the battle of Cowpens. He seems to have been just grown up at that time, and to have taken the field after the fall of Charleston, and to have kept it till the close of the war. He was the son of Wm. Hughes, and raised on Broad river near McCool's Ferry. After the war, he married Sarah Wright owned the tract of land now owned by Mrs. S. Gist at Scaufe's Ferry. He sold out many years ago and moved to Alabama.

Col. John Thomas, Sr., is said to have been a native of Wales, but brought up in Chester County, Penn. He married Jane Black in Penn's., removed to S. C,, and lived for a while on Fishing Creek, thence removed to Fairforest Creek. He was an Episcopalian, but his wife was a zealous Presbyterian. Before the Revolution, Thomas was a Captain and a magistrate under the Royal government. When Col. Thomas Fletchfall refused to hold a commission under the State government, an election was held, and John Thomas was chosen Colonel, he having previously resigned his commissions under the King. He commanded the Spartan regiment till near the time of the fall of Charleston, when he was succeeded by his son, John. The old man took protection, in hopes of being allowed to remain at home; but was arrested in 1780 and confined at Ninety Six, and subsequently at Charleston. After the war he removed to Greenville District. He had nine children.

1st.—John Thomas, Jr., who married a daughter of James McIlwaine, commanded the Spartan regiment for a time, and was then a Colonel in the State Troops.

2nd.—Capt. Robert Thomas, who fell in Roebuck's battle, March, 1781.

3rd.—Abraham Thomas, who died a prisoner at Ninety Six or Charleston, about the 1st of 1781.

4th.—Wm. Thomas, young in the time of the war, but distinguished on several occasions.

5th.—Martha Thomas, married to Josiah Culbertson in 1774. Culbertson, her husband, was valiant in battle and a captain before the war closed.

6th.—Ann Thomas, married to Maj. Jos. McFunkin, March 9th, 1779.

7th.—Jane Thomas, wife of Capt. Jos. McCool.

8th.—Letitia Thomas, wife of Maj. James Lusk.

9th.—Mrs. Carter, wholly unknown to me until very recently.

The posterity of Josiah Culbertson has probably beat that of Daniel Boone in killing game in the western wilds. One of his sons remained in this District, and may have descendants here.

Col. Roebuck's father lived on Tyger river, below the burnt factory. He moved from Virginia in 1777. His son, Benjamin, served as a Lieutenant in the company of Capt. Wm. Smith, in the expedition to Savannah, in 1779, and in other campaigns. He was made a Major in 1780, while absent in N. C., was in most of the battles of that year.

When John Thomas, Jr., joined the State Troops, he succeeded him in the command of the Spartan regiment, which he commanded at the Cowpens. Roebuck was taken by the Tories and put in jail for a time. His father died in Camden jail of smallpox. Col. Roebuck did good service aided by Lieut. Col. White. Col. Wm. Farr lived on Broad river, near Fish Dam Ford

Just before the fall of Charleston, Capt. Charles Sims came from Albemarle Co., Va., and settled on Tyger river at the mouth of Tinker creek. He was compelled to carry his family off, to be out of the reach of the Tory depredations. They stopped at the house of Rev. Joseph Alexander, D. D., in York District. A Mr. McDaniel married a daughter of Capt. Sims. Mrs. M. Jeter, still living, is another daughter. Wm. Sims Sr., son of Capt. Chas. Sims, lived many years on Broad river. The father of Wm. Sims, of Simstown, James S. Sims, of Pacolet, Knight Sims, and the late Clough S. Sims, and Mrs. Thompson.

John Rogers, father of Hon. James Rogers, was an Irishman, who lived and raised his family near the line of Newberry, between Tyger and Enoree.

In 1780, Col Patrick Moore, (a Tory) built a fort on the waters of Thicketty creek, which was a place of resort and protection for Tory hands, who went out in different directions to gather plunder, drive in cattle and collect horses,—extending their operations to the Whigs on Tinker creek, so that women and children were often without clothing, shoes, bread, meat or salt.

HUGHES FAMILY.—Two brothers of the names of Richard and Wm. Hughes came into the Union District Country, at an early period, and owned the land on the west side of the Broad river from below the mouth of Hughes' creek to Fannin's creek. They were natives of Wales, came first to Maryland, thence to S. C., both Whigs, both had families, and both lost their lives in the war.

Col. Steen's wife was a Bogan,—sister to Sam'l McFunkin's wife. Steen was killed in the summer of 1780, in Rowan Co., N. C. in an attempt to arrest some Tories.

As early as 1755, James Otterson resided in Tyger river, a short distance above Hamilton's ford. Maj. S. Otterson was his son, and one of the first elders of the Cane Creek Church.

In 1755, Sam'l McFunkin, Esq., was compelled to leave his home in Cumberland County, Pa., immediately after Braddock's defeat. With many others in like circumstances he moved south, or stopped on Tinker's creek. (Union Dist., S. C.) Dec. 24th.,—four miles from the present site of Unionville. He was a native of Ireland, but married a Miss Bogan in Penn'a. His son Maj. Jos. McFunkin was born June, 1755. S. McFunkin was a soldier in the war with the Cherokees commencing in 1760. Was a Presbyterian,—a decided Whig in the Revolution; and was a prisoner with Cornwallis, with Col. Hopkins and Capt. Jamieson, at the time of the battle of the Cowpens. He was a member of the Legislature which met in Jacksonboro, and advocated the confiscation act with all his powers. He was an elder in the Presbyterian church at Brown's creek. In his old age he sold his plantation, and died in Kentucky while moving to his youngest son in Indiana. His sons, Joseph and Dan'l McFunkin, were efficient soldiers in the Revolutionary war.

COL. THOS. BRANDON.—George Brandon, the father of Col. Thos. Brandon, lived on Tinker Creek, a strict Presbyterian. Col. T. Brandon lived in the time of the war 2 miles from Union C. H., near where Ellis now lives. John Brandon lived near W. Kennedy, on land now owned by his grandson, Benj. Brandon. He was there prior to 1764. Thos. Young, son-in-law of George Brandon, settled near his brother-in-law, Col. Thos. Brandon, about 1764. He had previously resided in Laurens District, and his son, John, was killed at Brandon's defeat, and Thos. turned soldier forthwith.

JOLLY FAMILY.—Time of their coming not known. Lived on Tinker Creek. John married Sarah Palmer, rose to the rank of Lieutenant, and was killed at Leighton's, on Fairforest, 1780.

BENJAMIN JOLLY rose to the rank of Major before the close of the war, was active in service and in most of the battles. He was engaged to be married, but died before the day appointed (evidently in 1781. L. C. D.) I have heard a tradition, that he had received a ring from his betrothed. This ring, a very remarkable one, was hid in a trunk, with money and other valuables, in the woods. Two Tories getting some knowledge of the whereabouts of the trunk, agreed to hunt it and divide the contents. The one who found it, refused to divide, and the other told the Whigs of the transaction after the death of Jolly. It is further said that the thief finally gave the ring to one of his daughters, and she wore it and died a miserable old maid, professing a general contempt for the whole of mankind; and, it is added, that one of her nieces now owns the ring, and though married bids fair to die childless.

GEN. ELIJAH CLARKE.—It is said that the Grindal Shoal, on Pacolet, tract of land was granted to Gen. Elijah Clark.

Wm. Hodges resided on Pacolet, two miles above the shoal. Tarleton went to his house just after the battle of Blackstocks, took him, and burnt his house, killed his stock, and sent him to Camden jail. He cut out the grating from a window with a pocket-knife, and he, Dan'l McFunkin and some others, passed the guards and made their escape.

COL. JAMES LITTLE.—The blockhouse at Cherokee ford, Savannah river, was under the command of Capt. James Little, at the time that Col. Boyd came to it. Little was a native of Virginia. His wife a Hamilton. He once resided at Long Cane, but prior to the war had moved over on Nan's (?) (Van's) Creek, in Georgia. You will find his name several times in McCall's Georgia. He commanded the blockhouse as above stated; had left ten men, and gone with the balance on a scout into Georgia. When they got word that the Tories were coming, they made "the canoe whiz till they got over." He refused Boyd's demands, and when the Tories left, he crossed the river and attacked them while landing from their rafts on the other side. He also gave notice to Anderson who was not far off, of what was passing. He went on to Kettle creek, etc. He was with Clark in his battles afterwards in this State (S. C.). He moved, about 1792, into what is now Franklin Co., Georgia, where a small stream bears the name. He died in April, 1807.

Having mentioned Col. Little, I may also state that I have reason to believe that a very clever officer was in the service in the region of Abbeville who spelled his name *Liddle* or *Liddel*. Some confusion might arise from confounding the names. Some of the posterity of Col. J. Little may be found on Little's Creek, Franklin Co., Georgia; of Mr. Liddel, at Decatur, Georgia. Be sure and ferret out what the Liddels did. Rev. D. Humphreys knows. Rev. D. Humphreys knows the present generation with that which has passed away.

Mr. Saye took notes of Maj. Jos. McFunkin, Maj. Thos. Young, C. Brandon, Maj. John Jefferies, Wm. Sims, Sr., Mrs. Angelica Nott, Sam'l Smith, Amos Lee and others.

HARMON GEIGER, one of the first settlers on the Congaree, was residing there about 1750, an experienced and much-respected Catawba Indian trader.

GEN. ROBERT ANDERSON was born in Staunton Co., Va., (Augusta Co.?) His parents came from Ireland. He settled in Abbeville District some time before the Revolution; married a Miss Thompson; removed to Pendleton District. He was a member of the Presbyterian church, and an elder for some 25 or 30 years, good tempered and very kind in his family, hospitable and courteous to his friends, lively and fond of anecdote, but rebuked with severity, when the laws of his God or country were trampled on.

He had no command during the war, but commanded a company in his District, and was prompt to bring delinquents to justice. He at times addressed this company publicly, and spoke well. Was a member of the State Legislature for several times while it was held in Charleston, and took part in the debates of that body. He died in 1812. His papers fell into the hands of his only son, Col. Robert Anderson; and the latter's son, Robert, now at Orange Springs, Fla., I imagine has them.

Gen. Anderson was a very good physician, practicing gratis among the poor.

He, as well as Gen. Pickens, was held in great veneration by the Cherokees. They always called both by the same name —Sky-gusta, great man. His eldest child, Mary, and Gen.

Pickens' daughter, Mary, were about the same age, and performed exploits when only 13 or 14 years of age that would have secured a laurel wreath for grown-up men of our day. They rode from one point of danger to another as expresses, assisted in the harvest field during the day, and wove at the loom at night to assist their mothers in clothing their families. Mary Anderson married first Mr. Maxwell, and then Mr. Carrouth, and proved herself a very superior woman.

GEN. ANDREW PICKENS.—Was born in Pennsylvania, but his parents came early from Ireland. He settled where Abbeville C. H. now stands, and aided in building the Long Cane church, near Abbeville C. H. After the war he moved to Pendleton District, settled a farm on the Seneca and called his place Hopewell. It was one mile above Gen. Anderson's. They both assisted in building the old Stone Church, 2 miles from Pendleton, where rest the remains of a great many of the first settlers and their families. It is one of the oldest churches in the upper part of the State.

Gen. Pickens remained here until all his sons and daughters were married, except his youngest son; and after the death of his wife, he removed to the mountains, and chose a quiet retreat near Tomassee, where he lived alone with his servants, except when one of his grandchildren would spend a while with him. It was not far from this spot that he fought one of his hardest battles with the Indians; but no one with whom I have conversed can tell me any of the particulars of that battle.

The Indians feared Sky-gusta greatly; and as he and Gen. Anderson were both county judges, he alminstered justice promptly.

Gen. Pickens' manners were mild. He was grave and taciturn. Was a member of the Presbyterian church, and elder at the Stone church, and also at Bethel, a little church in the mountains. He was faithful in training his family for heaven—kpt up family worship regularly—and retired every day to a room alone for secret prayer.

The Indians remembered the two old Generals with the greatest veneration years after their death; when their children or grandchildren would pass through the nation, they would not charge them, but would entertain them hospitably, and when they would enquire who they were, would say, they could make them pay: "Children of Sky-gusta, they Red Man's friend, they more than welcome."

Gen. Pickens died at Tamossee in the summer of 1817 (I think). His remains rest in the church yard of the old Stone church All of his children are dead except his youngest daughter in Alabama.

Gen. Pickens' eldest daughter, Mary, was married to Squire John Harris, who died in April, 1845, aged 83. Mrs. Harris and her early friend, Mary Anderson, both lived to a venerable old age.

The above sketches of Gen'ls. Anderson and Pickens, written by A. T. Harris, Seneca, Nov. 24, 1857.

Raneage says a Catawba Indian, whom the Whigs called Monday, was often with his company in the battles with the Tories, British and Cherokees. He was with them at the "Whig fight" and did them great service. Sometime after, when everything seemed lost to the Whig cause, Monday fell into a state of dejection, knowing if the cause failed, he must suffer; under the circumstances he hung himself at Ninety Six.

A *memo.* on the cover of the newspaper from which I copy the preceding says "Dr. J. Winsmith, Spartanburg, near Glenn Springs"—and in the paper he is once spoken of as "Dr." and once as "Hon." J. Winsmith. L. C. D.

At Greenwood, S. C., July 21 to July 29th, 1871.

CAPT. WM. BEAL, OF NINETY SIX REGION.—Shortly after Ninety Six fell into the hands of the British, Bloody Bill Cunningham's band of Tory marauders visited Mrs. Beal, the mother of the Captain, for the purpose of plundering. On entering the house, they demanded in the most peremptory terms all the money and valuable articles she possessed; she quickly complied, and surrendered everything, even to the uttermost farthing. Cunningham pretended to be dissatisfied, and said she had retained a part. She solemnly declared she had not. Having removed everything desirable, Cunningham before leaving drew his sword and chopped Mrs. Beal across one arm, the scar of which remained to the day of her death, which occurred many years after peace.

Capt. Beal's indignation was fired to the highest pitch, and he determined to have revenge. He accordingly set out in quest of those ruffians who had plundered the house of his widowed mother in his absence, and did not go far before he met with the conspicuous Tory on Wilson's creek who had been the principal actor. They immediately recognized each other, as they had been acquainted for several years. Beal rushed towards the Tory in a furious manner, who put spurs to his horse and soon had him to the top of his speed, flying from death. After running their horses about three miles, the Tory drew a pistol and shot Beal's horse dead from under him. He then halted and considered whether he should charge on Beal or not. Beal took his pistol from his holsters and retreating dared the Tory to come on; but the Tory knowing him to be a swamp fox, and fearing that he might have a party of Whigs in ambush, concluded that it was best to abandon the project, particularly as Beal defied him in such a gallant manner. Beal stated that he could have shot the Tory several times, but preferred putting him to death with his sword.

In a few days after this transaction, young Beal met with his antagonist on Saluda river. They spoke to each other as courteously as if they had been mutual friends, and the Tory very politely invited Beal to come over. Beal asked him if he would remain there till he came. He replied in the affirmative. Beal then plunged into the river, and when he had swam about half across the stream, the Tory bade him good morning and rode off in great haste, promising to see him some other time.

It was not long, however, before Beal had occasion to visit the house of a friend some distance below Cambridge, which he did, accompanied by a Whig. When they arrived at the place, they dismounted and tied their horses very close to the door, there being but one door to the house. After remaining a short space of time, a large company was heard riding up, which they were confident must be Tories. "What shall we do?" said Beal's comrade. "Do as I tell you," replied Beal, "and I think you are safe. The night is dark and they cannot see us. Rush to your horse, rattle your sword, and make as great noise as possible, and I have no doubt we can put them to flight." This they both did, and Beal called in a very loud voice for his men to parade, as if he were commanding a regiment. The Tories instantly halted. The Whigs then rode towards them, and Beal cried out: "If you are soldiers, stand and prove it." The Tories, fearing that they were about to be attacked by superior numbers, quickly retreated in great confusion. It was afterwards ascertained that there were thirteen in the company, under the immediate command of Bill Cunningham. The Tories were mortified when they subsequently learned that they had been put to flight by two men.

Capt. Beal resided for many years near old Cambridge, and subsequently removed to and died in Georgia, where he was greatly respected.

(Writer's name not given):

MAJ. WM. DUNLAP, born July 25th, 1765; died Dec. 20, 1838; aged 73. In early life engaged in the war of Independence; afterwards served in the Legislature of S. C. Pure and upright in his morals, faithful to every trust.

MAJ. JONATHAN DOWNS was in the fight at Williamson's Fort at Ninety Six, (Nov. 1775). His father-in-law, Capt. Wm. Gray, was killed—were famished for water.

KING'S MOUNTAIN.—I have to doubt that Campbell was elected by Shelby and Sevier their commander on the Catawba, above Gilbert Town. But the tradition of the country about King's Mountain always had been that Campbell was elected the morning before the battle was fought, by all the Colonels, viz.: Lacey, Hill, Cleveland, Williams, Shelby and Sevier. The tradition goes on to say that Williams being the oldest Colonel, was much offended that he was not elected commander; at first refused to go into the battle, and started off with his men; but hearing the firing as the battle began, he wheeled about and rushed into it and fought bravely until he was killed. I have no doubt there was first an election by Shelby and Sevier, and afterwards by all the Colonels near the battle ground."—Dr. M. D. Moore, Sept. 15, 1858.

CALHOUN FAMILY.—John N. Hutton, Hopewell, P. C., Greene Co., Ala., Nov. 13, 1858.

In the fall of 1759, four brothers of Calhouns migrated from Pennsylvania to Abbeville District, and settled on Calhoun's Creek and vicinity, in company with thirty other families. On the 18th Feb., 1760, hearing that they were going to be attacked by the Indians, left their home for Tobler's Fort, near Augusta, Ga.; but before reaching it, were overtaken by the savages, and several of their number slain.

The names of the four brothers were James, Ezekiel, William and Patrick. William was born in 1723; married Agnes Long, March 19, 1749, who was born in 1733, and had eleven children. Two of their daughters were killed by the Indians, and a third one captured and kept two years. Another, Nancy, married Gen. Jos. Hutton, ancestor of the writer.

In a ms. sketch of Jos. Griffin, a Revolutionary soldier, of Laurens, by Bethiah S. East, it is stated that Col. Jos. Hayes was in Musgrove's Mill battle, under whom Griffin served there.

HAYES' MASSACRE.—Cunningham told Hayes' men that if they would come out of the house and lay down their arms, they should be treated as prisoners of war. After some consultation, they complied. Cunningham marched them out into the old field, and after attempting to hang two on a stock pole, which broke, ordered them to sit down on the ground, took his sword and went to hacking them up and down until his fiendish malice was satisfied with the groans of the mangled and dying, when he told his men to complete the bloody work. Jos. Griffin, who belonged to Hayes' company of forty men stationed there, had been sent off on an express the previous day. The house had been fired, and they were compelled to yield.

KING'S MOUNTAIN.—Old Drury Mathis was at the battle of King's Mountain, and was severely wounded in the thigh. He had enlisted and gone there with Ferguson from Saluda Old Town. He afterwards reported that a large portion of Ferguson's native soldiers were from the Ninety Six District, and principally from the vicinity of Old Ninety Six. He received his wound in the third charge, which was against Campbell down the Northern side of the mountain towards the rivulet. His position on falling was near the middle of the declivity where the balls from the mountaineers fell as thick as hail. In the succeeding charges, the Britons and mountain men alternately passed over him—the former charged over him down the mountain; the latter went pushing up to renew the attack. He says he could see the faces and eyes of the mountaineers as they passed him. They appeared like so many devils from the infernal regions, and charged like enraged lions upon the enemy. He says, too, they were the most powerful looking men he ever beheld. They were not fat but tall, raw-boned, sinewy, with long matted hair—such men as were never before seen in these parts. He says he placed himself with his head toward the Tories, who were overshooting the mark, and his feet down the mountain, and if ever a poor fellow hugged Mother Earth closely he did it then. After the battle Mathis was taken to some house in the neighborhood, and nursed till his wound had healed, when he returned to Ninety Six.

It is still traditionary, that the beautiful branch that winds around the Northern side of the mountain was crimsoned with blood the day of the battle. It was repeatedly across it that Campbell and his dauntless men were driven before the bayonets of the British, and as often returned to the charge.

their deadly rifles making awful havoc in the ranks of the retiring enemy. The little flat there, and the branch itself, were soon drawn to the spot by the smell of the blood, and many of the wounded as could, dragged themselves to this water to slake their intolerable thirst, or to wash the blood from their bodies. The wolves of the surrounding country were soon drawn to the spot by the smlel of the blood, and for two months they revelled upon the dead bodies that strewed the mountain and its ravines. Long after the war, it is said to have been a favorite haunt of the wolf hunters. The taste of human flesh made them fierce and abundant.

Williams and Ferguson fell nearly at the same time, on the Eastern side of the mountain. Williams from a more elevated and favorable position than those occupied by Campbell or Hambright, saw the magic influence of Ferguson's whistle. Dashing to the front, his horse throwing bloody foam from his mouth that had been struck by a ball, he was heard to exclaim: "I'll silence that whistle, or die in the attempt." Quickly Ferguson was no more, and soon after a ball from the enemy laid Williams mortally wounded on the hillside. Hambright, who lived in the vicinity, spent the night in the standing tents of the enemy, surrounded with the dead and dying.* The mountain men, immediately after the battle, took teh same trail they had come, and retreated with their prisoners and arms, from the mountain. They carried with them also Col. Williams and the other wounded Whigs.

The Mountaineers, on their return, stopped near the house of Jacob Randall, who lived on High Shoals Creek, a branch of Kings. It was here Williams expired, after a draught of water from the hands of Silas Randall. This was the old King's Mountain and Cherokee Ford Road. Ferguson's mistress, Virginia Poll, was the first to fall in the battle.

SIEGE OF NINETY SIX.—Capt. Carr, of the British army, was in all the actions of the South during the Revolution.

---

*Something seems to be here omitted. Hambright was badly wounded. I copy it as I find it. L. C. D.

He was at the siege of Ninety Six, where he says that two days before the retreat of Greene, a council of war had been called in the fort, a respectable minority voted to hold out till the next day. Next day another council was held at which every man voted to surrender, except a young Lieutenant; and it was determined to hold out that day. Next morning another council was held, when the same lieutenant begged that they would hold out till that afternoon, when they would surrender. They did so, when John Caldwell rode in under the fire of the Americans with a letter from Rawdon in his hand. He had been paid one hundred guineas by the British for this service. He afterwards removed to Georgia, and there died at an advanced age.

GEN. ANDREW WILLIAMSON had two daughters, Mary Ann and Eliza. Mary married first a Mr. Walker; after his death, Judge Ephraim Ramsey, by whom she had the following children: Sallie, David and Richard. By Walker she had two, Eliza and Agnes Keller.

Eliza Williamson married Charles Goodwin by whom she had Dr. Chamberlain, Eliza, Annie and Charles. Mrs. Chamberlain Goodwin is still living near Edgefield, C. H. She was a Miss Gray. Anna married a Mr. Beggs, of Beach Island. Beggs killed himself drinking. Mrs. Beggs raised a large family, all of whom did well. She still lives. Eliza married Henry Tutt, and removed to Barnwell or Beach Island, and probably still lives.

BRANDON'S DEFEAT.

BY THOMAS YOUNG.

The scene of Brandon's defeat is four miles South of Unionville on waters of Fairforest. He had stopped to take a check at the head of a large hollow. The Tories were led by one Adam Stidham. The Whigs being taken by surprise, ran without striking a blow. It was a complete rout. Brown, a half brother of Gen. Morgan, was killed; also one of the Scotts and John Young. Old Samuel Clowney, Colonel Clowney's father, said he didn't put the bit in his beast's mouth, but mounted him, and whipped out of the way. Brown was buried on the spot near the place where the widow Polly Young now lives. It is near the road, Maj. Young in his lifetime pointed out the very spot; a bush grew up from the grave, and he requested that it should never be cut down.

BRANDON was not altogether free from blame in this affair. He was brave, but seemed to be too careless for a good officer. He was sometimes charged with cruelty. Brandon lies buried four miles East of Union C. H. at the spot then known as Brown's Creek Presbyterian Church. The church has since been removed to the village. He was buried with military honors. A horse was accoutred as for battle, with holsters, pistols, sword, and even his military boots in the stirrups. The military were out in full force. In person he was chunky and compactly built. Thomas was his given name. He was uncle to Maj. Thomas Young; and father of Thomas, William and James, and a daughter named Jane, and another Ann, and still another Elizabeth. They have all left the State. At the battle of Cowpens, as an instance of his humanity, his nephew, Thomas Young, who was but a boy and had just joined Washington the night before, was approached by a stalwart British dragoon; Brandon saw his danger, and galloping up, struck up his sword and killed the Briton. Tom Young was placed in that battle behind a Frenchman who had served in Pulaski's Legion, who proved himself a most capital swordsman. Seeing the youth of Young, he said to him, "Don't be scared, my son; I can cut my way through the British columns at any time," and he could do it.

SAM CLOWNEY was once sent to a ford on Fairforest above Union to watch and report the Tories that might pass. Five came into the creek, and conceiving himself equal to them, he shouted as if commanding a dozen men, "Cock your guns, boys, and fire at the word," and approaching them, deliberately ordered them to lay down their arms. The Tories believing a large force upon them, complied without a word—handed him their guns, which he laid upon the ground, resumed his own, and then ordered them to march to the Whig camp. He was asked after he arrived safely there, how he managed to take them. "Why, by me faith, I surrounded them." Clowney was a member of the old Brown's Creek Church. The personal description given of him was, that he was a little dry Irishman. He possessed a remarkable talent for sarcasm and invective; but he was a most kind-hearted, benevolent man, beloved by all who knew him. Like all his race of that day, without being an intemperate man, he loved a wee bit occasionally. His brogue was quite rich, and this combined with a fund of genial Irish wit made him a fascinating companion. He was the father of Hon. Wm. K. Clowney. His wife was a sister of Rev. John B. Kennedy.

A Tory named Wm. Lee, who lived on Tyger, in Union, committed many depredations, and among them robbed the mother of Thos. Young. At the close of the war he left the country.

From the neighborhood of Gossett's Mills, on Enoree, a Scotchman named Ross, a Tory, ran away at the close of the war. He went to the Cherokee nation, and when going down the Tennessee river with goods for New Orleans, he was taken by a party of Indians, and would have been killed, if his life had not been interceded for by a young Indian girl, whom he afterwards married, and a son, John Ross, of this marriage, became chief of the nation.

The Ottersons lived on Tyger, North side near a place known as Cook's Mills. At Sam Otterson's house was the fort known as Otterson's Fort. It was here that the people of Union, and a part of Laurens, found protection from the Indians.

Alexander Shaw writes from Horn Lake, Miss., Sept. 27, 1858: Says he lived near the Indian line of S. C., near Col.

Cleveland's." "I became acquainted with Horse Shoe Robinson, who lived on the farm called Horse Shoe, on a creek called Changee. I travelled many hundred miles with him about the year 1825. We both moved to Alabama, near Tuscaloosa. There he died, leaving three sons, who were steady, sober, consistent citizens. I have not known them for many years. I often heard Robinson relate many things that are now set forth in the novel called Horse Shoe Robinson, and many others also. So that work is founded on fact, and is truly characteristic of him. General Pinckney visited our region, had a farm there, and recognized Robinson as an active soldier at the siege of Charleston and a ready bearer of dispatches. Pinckney paid great attention to Robinson.

JAMES WARDLAW's statement:

MUSGROVE'S MILL.—At Musgrove's Mill, whilst the firing was going on across the river, Sam Moore led a party of twelve men up the river and across, and rushed down upon the enemy with such force as to put them to flight. Of this affair I have heard chlidren of Col. Syles speak.

GEN. ROBERT IRWIN.—His sister Mary (who married Wm. Blackstock) and others, being all children of Wm. Irwin, of West Pennsbury, Cumberland Co., Pa., said Wm. Irwin died prior to May, 1763—these and other heirs sell their undivided right to 100 acres of land to John Irwin in said West Pennsbury for 15 each. Blackstock signs his name with his mark "B," in behalf of his wife. The above, "all of Cumberland Co., Pa.," showing they all still resided there in May and June, 1763, the dates on the paper.

LOCHABER.—The tract of land called Lochaber, was on Penny's Creek, in Abbeville District. Alexander Cameron lived on and owned it—the Cherokee agent.

GEN. ROBERT IRWIN.—Gen. Irwin, Mecklenburgh, Sept. 19, 1781, writes his brother, Capt. John Irwin, saying: "I am to set out for camp this day against the Scotch and British at Cross Creek; for although we have several offers of peace, upon certain terms, yet our country is invaded, and the surest way to restore peace on good terms is by a rigorous exertion at this critical time."

HAUK'S DEFEAT.—Traditions of Starr Moore.

The Whigs had about 150 men. One mile and a half from the house of Samuel Williamson, they divided into two divisions—one was led by Capt. John McClure, and the other by Capt. Wm. Bratton. McClure marched through a field. With Bratton there was a drunken soldier whose impetuosity somewhat hastened matters—he would press too far forward. The first man killed was the sentinel, first reached by Bratton's division. The sentinel was fast asleep. Sam Williamson was left to guard him, with an injunction to shoot him if he should stir. He soon did so, and was shot by Williamson. Then both parties (McClure and Bratton's) raised the war whoop, as they had agreed upon, and rushed to the attack.

As soon as McClure reached the crib, he released those who were prisoners (imprisoned in the crib)—they were Tom Clendennin, Robert Bratton, and John Moore. Moore had pushed off the top of the crib, and gave a hurra for the Whigs, when one of the guard raised his gun to shoot him, and was prevented by the Captain of the guard. David Saddler was guide to McClure at this point. He afterwards married Col. Bratton's eldest daughter. John Carroll killed Hauk from a clump of plum trees. Old James Williamson, father of Sam Williamson, had come from Pennsylvania; they were Scotch-Irish. He had five sons. Dr. Sam Williamson, President of Davidson, was his grandson, and son of Samuel, also Lauder Williamson, of Lancaster.

The place is now owned by Mrs. J. S. Bratton. Only one Whig was killed or wounded—a man named Campbell, of Chester. He had taken a prisoner, and carried him to the house; but as he turned away, the fellow drew a pistol from his clock, shot Campbell dead, and made his escape.

When this battle took place, Hauk had come up into this Fishing Creek settlement to offer the people protection. Ferguson had gone up by Ninety Six. McClure and Bratton were retreating towards Charlotte, when a runner overtook them and informed them of the depredations of Hauk. They resolved to return and give him battle. They numbered first about 200, but soon dropped off to 150, under a forced march to the enemy. Hauk was at this encamped at Walker's Cross Road, 8 miles from Williamson's, now called Lewis' Turn Out, on the Charlotte railroad.

JOHN MOORE, JR., was sent forward to scout, and find out the position and strength of Hauk; he met a mill-boy before reaching Walker's Cross Roads, who told him of Hauk's removal up to the vicinity of Capt. Bratton's; there was a strong neighborhood of Whigs there. He now returned to the Saluda road, and overtook them, they had come so rapidly as to pass him. As they had marched along, numerous friends had persuaded them (the Americans) not to undertake it. At old Wm. Adair's, in Chester, the old man and lady took hold of John Adair, their son, and detained him by force; he watched his chance, and springing from them, mounted his horse, and soon overtook the command, leaving his mother screaming. John Adair afterwards went to Kentucky. In the days of Nullification, true to his blood and his beloved native State, he returned to South Carolina, and solicited the command of a regiment—he was then seventy.

When Hauk approached Williamson's and Capt. Bratton's, he found Mrs. Bratton in the field with her reapers taking wheat. Bob Bratton was here taken prisoner, and perhaps Clendennen. Hauk put the reap-hook around Mrs. Bratton's neck, and threatened to cut off her head, when Adamson, his second in command, interfered and prevented it. Adamson, afterwards, in urging his horse over a ditch, he fell and threw him, and he was taken. They were about to dispatch him, when he begged to see Mrs. Bratton. She instantly recognized him, and begged his life, which was granted. Adamson lived in 1807 in Camden—he was a Loyalist.

They hitched their horses a mile and a quarter from the field of battle. They got their information of the enemy's position from two young men, Wm. Moore and Isaac Ball—Moore was a brother of John M. N. Ball, was a nephew of Sam Rainey.

LACEY joined them on the way, and acted in the fight as a private. Winn was with the Whigs at Hauk's defeat, as a private.

The encampment of Bratton and McClure, 8 miles from Charlotte, was on the plantation of a Mrs. Smart.

HILL'S IRON WORKS BURNED.—One John Dennis was the Tory who guided the British to the burning of Hill's Works.

Old Gum-Log Moore's house was built on Fishing Creek, some 20 feet from the water; often it was surrounded with water. Wm. Adair's house, also old Richard Saddler's, stood in the same way. They were built thus to be as safe as possible from the lurking Cherokees, who often waylaid them while going for water, or when washing.

The names of the old settlers in this neighborhood of Fishing Creek, were Wm. Bratton, James Williamson, John Moore, Sam Rainey, Richard Saddler, father of David, Wm. Clendenen, Tom Bratton, older brother of William; Sam Williamson, he had married a Miss Starr, aunt of Mr. Starr Moore, of York; Thom. Black, Rev. John Simpson, some six miles lower in Chester; James Moore, grandfather of Dr. Maurice Moore, of Glenn Springs, and Dr. Wm. Moore, of York. These people worshipped in Bethesda, in York, and Fishing Creek Church in Chester.

Col. Bratton was buried at Bethesda.

JAMES MOORE was also at Hauk's defeat; he was the father of Philander Moore, of the same neighborhood of Bethesda.

Tom Black's place is now owned by the Miss Rowells and a Williamson.

On Bullock's Creek were the Meeks, three of whom, Moses, James and Adam were in the war. The place is still owned by the grandson; Mr. Starr Moore owns now Adam Meek's place. The McElwees, three in the war, James, John and William, all brave men—John and William lie buried near King's Mountain at Old Bethany; John was a most noble fellow. The Chambers—their place is now owned by Galbraith Caldwell, the Retters, and Isaac McElwee. The Allisons— old Robt. Allison—Sam Turner—Robt. T. Allison, is his son. The Jamisons, James and John, were most true Whigs. The Shearers, and the Feemsters, John and James, good Whigs. Capt. Roberts, as brave a man as ever lived. The Barnetts, Humphrey and Jacob; they and Roberts all belonged to a horse company. James Meek was a Captain in the Revolution.

Gen. Samuel McGowen, of Abbeville, S. C., in a published address before the literary societies of Erskine College, Abbeville, August 8, 1855, says, speaking of the Cherokee outbreak in 1776: "Capt. Aaron Smith's family on Little River, consisting of fifteen souls, male and female, white and black, had all been massacred, except two sons; one of these had escaped to White Hall, and alarmed that settlement whilst the other, hard-pressed by barbarians thirsting for his blood, had succeeded in reaching the residence of Mr. Francis Salvador, on Coranaca Creek, and there holding up the bleeding stumps of his mutilated hands, told the fearful tale of the slaughter, and roused the scattered settlers of that vicinity to rally, for the double purpose of avenging their murdered neighbors, and of protecting their own firesides and families.

"This irruption of the Indians upon the Western border of the Province, was doubtless intended to be simultaneous with the attack on Charleston and the seaboard; and on the morning of the day rendered ever memorable by the declaration of American Independence, DeWitt's Corner was deserted —Major Downes, and the people of Rabun's Creek, were besieged by the Cherokees at Langley's Fort on the Saluda—and Col. Williamson and Mr. Salvador, with a muster of militia, hastily collected and still collecting, lay at Holmes' field on Hogskin Creek. This little army of mliitia soon crossed the border and burnt most of the lower towns, among which was Esseneca, where the lamented Salvador fell, and was brutally scalped by the ruthless enemy. It also penetrated into the middle settlements and valleys, and inflicted upon the whole nation of Cherokees, including the over-hills, such signal chastisoment that they sued for peace, and concluded a treaty with South Carolina and Georgia, by which they acknowledged themselves vanquished, and ceded to South Carolina all the territory lying on this side of the Oconee Mountain. This treaty was made by representatives of the different parties, in May, 1777, and if by a sort of poetical justice, was signed at DeWitt's Corner, near the place where the war had been commenced by indiscriminate massacre and midnight murder."

KING'S MOUNTAIN.—From the South Carolinian, (Columbia).

"Montcalm, near Aburgon, Va., March 16, 1857.

My Dear Sir:—The day you spent part of with us, in conversation about the battle of King's Mountain, you asked me if I knew the route taken by the volunteers under Col. Wm. Campbell, from the Sycamore Shoals, or flats on Watauga, across the mountains into South Carolina, in pursuit of Ferguson. I told you I had a statement showing the route, somewhere among my papers. Since you were here, I have found it. It was copied by myself from a manuscript journal kept by Ensign Robert Campbell, and is as follows:

"In the expedition to King's Mountain, Col. Campbell, Col. Shelby, and Col. Sevier rendezvoused at the Sycamore flats, on Wautauga, at the foot of Yellow Mountain on the 25th of Sept., 1780. Next day they ascended the mountain, mostly on horseback, and encamped at night in the gap of the mountain on the opposite side. The ascent over this part of the mountain was not very difficult. There was a road, but not one on which wagons could pass. No provisions were taken, but such as each man could carry in his wallet or saddle-bags. The sides and top of the mountain were covered with snow, shoe-mouth deep. On the top of the mountain there was about 100 acres of beautiful table land in which a spring issued, ran through it, and over into Wautauga. Here the volunteers paraded.

On reaching the plain beyond the mountain, they found themselves in a country covered with verdure, and breathed an atmosphere of summer mildness. The second night (the night of the 27th), they rested at Cuthay's plantation. The third day they fell in with Gen. McDowell, and that night held a consultation of the officers. The General was without troops—yet his rank and former services could not easily be overlooked. It was stated in the council that they needed an experienced officer to command them. Morgan was the man they wanted, and to obviate all difficulties, Gen. McDowell offered to be the bearer of their wishes to Gen. Cates. The fourth night (the 29th), they rested at a rich Tory's, where they obtained abundance of every necessary refreshment. On the fifth day (the 30th), they reached the Catawba, where they were joined by Gen. Cleveland. Here they dispatched Gen. McDowell to Gen. Cates."

This is as far as I copied from Col. Robt. Campbell's manuscript. I have, however, this further memorandum:

The battle was fought on Saturday, the 7th of October. On the next Saturday, a court-martial was held for the trial of certain prisoners charged with various offences.

I have no account of the movements each day of the forces after the 20th of September, up to the 7th of October, further than what is stated in the official account.

Most truly your friend,

DAVID CAMPBELL.

List of officers in command of Col. Campbell's regiment:

Major—William Edmondson.

Captains—James Dysart, Robert Creig, Andrew Colvill, David Beatie, William Neil, Andrew Edmondson, and Wm. Edmondson.

Lieutenants commanding parts of Companies—Reece Bowen, Wm. Russell, and Thomas McColloch.

Lieutenants—Samuel Newell, Robert Edmondson, 2nd, and Wm. Crabtree.

Ensigns—Robert Campbell, James Corry, Nathaniel Dryden, Humberson Lyon, James Laird, and Nathaniel Guist.

James Hames, Sr.,—(from the Rutherdton, N. C., Enquirer, Aug. 30, 1859).

He was born in Mecklenburg, Va.; entered the service at Union, S. C., in 1776; was then on the Cherokee campaign—at Blackstock's, Cowpen's, seige of Fort Granby, Ninety Six, and Entaw.

When Col. Henderson was severely wounded at Entaw Springs, Hames carried him on his back from the field to the camp.

When on a scouting expedition under Col. Brandon, fell in with Gen. Marion with his troops near Granby; unitedly followed and defeated a large body of Tories camped on the Pedee river, pursued them down Broad river, which was to be crossed by a bridge. Previous to passing over, General Marion ordered the soldiers to spread their blankets on the bridge, in order to prevent the Tories (who were supposed to be near) from hearing the tread of their horses. Before all had passed over, the Tories commenced the attack, but were repulsed, leaving behind several prisoners.

GEN. PICKENS.—After the struggle for our independence had terminated, our State Legislature thought it proper to pass a bill "to exempt from legal investigation the conduct of the militia while the war lasted." But so soon as the bill was proposed, Gen. Pickens said, like a noble Marion, "If, in a single instance, in the course of my command, I have done that which I cannot fully justify, justice requires that I should suffer for it."

GEN. JACKSON'S BIRTH PLACE.—South Carolina and Virginia have been disputing for some time past the honor of having given Gen. Jackson to the country. Whilst they have been talking, Gen. S. H. Walkup, of Union county, has been gathering facts and statistics to show that the old hero was born in that part of Mecklenburg, now Union.

The facts which he ascertained are stated in a letter to the Charlotte Democrat to this effect: Old Andrew Jackson, (father of Gen. Andrew Jackson, President of the United States), George McCamie or McKemey, James Crawford, John Leslie, Samuel Leslie and James Crow, all married sisters: Betty, Peggy, Jinny, Molly, Sally and Grace, whose maiden names were Hutchinson. The first two and Samuel Leslie settled about 1765 or 1766 in North Carolina; the other three in South Carolina. George McCamie and Sam Leslie lived within half a mile of each other, near Cureton's Pond, N. C. James Crawford and his brother Robert lived about two and a half miles from them, and in South Carolina, near each other. Old Andrew Jackson settled about ten miles from McCamie's, on Twelve Mile Creek, in North Carolina, where he died before the birth of his son Andrew. Crow and John Leslie settled about the same distance off in South Carolina.

After the death of Andrew Jackson, Sr., his widow left twelve Mile Creek to live with her friends in Waxhaws, and more particularly with the Crawfords, who were most wealthy. On her way there, from her residence on Twelve Mile Creek, she stopped at her sister's, Mrs. McCamie's, and was taken in labor and was delivered of Andrew Jackson, afterwards General and President of the United States. As soon as she recovered from her confinement at McCamie's, she took her son Andrew and proceeded to what is called the Wren place, about two and a half miles from McCamie's, in South Carolina, belonging to Crawford, and there remained with her son until he was taken to Crawford's residence, near Waxhaw Bridge, where he remained till about the close of the Revolutionary War.

The certificates establishing these facts are in Gen. Walkup's possession, and he proposes to publish them in proper form.—*Fayetteville Observer.*

GEN. ROBT. IRWIN.—Robt. A. Harris, Jr., to Capt. John Irwin, Aug. 15, 1778, says: "Your brother, Col. Irwin, is now at the Assembly of this State."

Traditions of Wm. Black, of York.—That Major Chronicle, well acquainted with the locality, suggested the mode of attack on Ferguson at King's Mountain—it was adopted—and his party on the right—Campbell in the centre—and Chronicle was the first to bring on the action, and was the first who fell, shot dead, as he neared the enemy, and raised his head to give the word to fire.

HON. ALEXANDER BOWRIE, Ben Lomond, Talladega, December 22, 1856.

"Of my deceased father his Revolutionary services, it does not become me to do more than give you a brief detail of facts, without comment. He was a Scotchman by birth, and emigrated to this country in 1762. On the 25th of Feb., 1776, he was commissioned a Captain in the Fifth Regiment raised in South Carolina, which was soon after put on the Continental establishment. In March, 1777, his company, with another commanded by Capt. Pitt, were by resolution of the Government and Council, detached from the Fifth Regiment and taken into the service of the State as independent companies. My father was engaged in the battle of Stone, acting in the capacity of Brigade Major of Williamson's Brigade. In this battle his first Lieutenant Prince was killed. He was also engaged in the storming of Savannah, where he again acted in the capacity of Brigade Major. He was also in the hard fought battle of Guilford, where being without a command, he acted as a volunteer aid of Gen. Huger. In the latter part of the war he was generally acting with Gen. Pickens.

GEN. ANDREW WILLIAMSON.—My information in regard to Gen. Williamson, is more full than in regard to any of the others, because in the early part of the war, and before it began, there existed between my father and him, a very close and intimate friendship. I have often heard from the lips of my revered father the melancholy story of Williamson's defection from the cause of his country.

General Williamson, although a Scotchman, was an illiterate man. He was able to write only his name, and that he learned to do mechanically, without any knowledge of the letters he was making. His manner of writing his name was WmSon. He was, nevertheless, by nature, a man of uncommon intellect. Before, and during a large portion of the Revolutionary War, he was a decided patriot and Whig. He held a high command in the Provincial militia, and his skill and bravery were undoubted.

His residence was near (or at) White Hall. My father was in the habit of dining with him frequently, and this hospitality was frequently reciprocated. Williamson's patriotism was, I believe, undoubted and unsuspected until after the capitulation of Ninety Six (Charleston?). This event seemed to all, except the boldest spirits, to be the end of the struggle in that part of South Carolina, if not in the whole State. The British regarded the country as not only conquered, but subdued. General Williamson was a man of considerable wealth, to which, as was not unnatural, he was much attached. But here I close the curtain. His motives, whatever they may have been, belong to him and his God.

I now continue the narrative, as near as possible, in the words of the narrator:

"Not long after the surrender and capitulation of Ninety Six, I received an invitation to dine with Gen. Williamson, at his own house, with the assurance that I should meet only a small party of particular friends. I went expecting to spend a social day with such Whig gentlemen as I had been accustomed to meet at his hospitable table. To my utter surprise and mortification, upon entering his parlor I found it crowded with British officers in full uniform. A moment's reflection determined me to submit to the exigencies of my position with the best grace I could command. After dinner, and after a very few glasses of wine, I arose from the table and took a respectful leave of the company; but after very plainly evincing to the watchful eye of Gen. Williamson my utter dissatisfaction with the whole affair.

"Within a day or two afterwards Gen. Williamson rode up to my house, and soon after invited me to take a walk with him. He commenced the conversation by referring to the dinner party at his house, and expressing his surprise and regret at my too evident displeasure on the occasion. I then very seriously addressed him as follows: 'You know, Gen. Williamson, that when you invited me to dine with you—a thing I had often done before—you said I was only to meet a few particular friends. I went without suspicion that any change had taken place in the political views of Gen. Williamson. You can well conceive my surprise, then, when instead of meeting such men as Col. Pickens, Mr. Rapley, and others of like stamp, I found your parlor filled with officers. I felt that all was not right, but determined to put the best face on the matter that I could. After the cloth was removed, and wine introduced, you requested your guests to fill their glasses, and to my utter confusion gave as the first toast 'the King!' Well, as I had no personal quarrel with King George, (so I satisfied my honor) I drank it, but in that glass I drank farewell to all further intercourse with Gen. Williamson. But this was not all. Immediately afterwards, intending your remark for my especial ear, you observed that you thought it now high time for every man in this country to choose which side he would espouse. I had long since made my choice, and I thought Gen. Wliliamson had made his. As soon as I could with decency I left the table and rode home.' He was evidently much disturbed by these remarks, and became affected even to tears. But he had gone too far to recede; and to the day of his death, I have no doubt, sorely lamented the fatal step he had taken."

After this, my recollection is that Gen. Williamson joined the British army, and never again associated with his old friends in the upper country. His estate, I believe, was confiscated by the South Carolina Legislature.

"Chester County—(Writer not given).

HANGING ROCK.—Col Davie at the battle of Hanging Rock, was heard to cry out in his loud voice to the Prince of Wales Regiment, "Soldiers, if you value your lives, ground your arms, and officers surrender at once." They continued, however, to fight with the usual sullenness of British soldiers.

It was here also that one of the Gaston boys (there were four of them) ran for a branch to slake his thirst, deeming himself desperately wounded—he could hear the blood spurting from his body on the leaves as he ran—he fell at the branch, with only strength to say to others who were drinking, "I am wounded and bleeding—stop the blood." On examination it was found that he was not bleeding, but a ball had pierced his powder-horn, which sent the powder in a jet, at every step, on the leaves. Such is imagination.

FISH DAM FORD.—The skirmish at Fish Dam was fought in Chester, in the flat on Broad River, between the ford and the ferry. A Mrs. Polly Crosby then lived there, who reported as many as twenty (British) killed, and many others wounded —some of them were nursed at her house—two died there, she buried on the hill near the house. Old Col. Hopkins took an active part in this battle.

SANDY RIVER SETTLEMENT.—This was on the West over Broad River portion of Chester—was mostly if not entirely Tories. Hopkins was perhaps the only exception. The people here, even in the Revolution, were all rich—had the best lands of the district and all the negroes—there is not now and never was a Presbyterian church among them. To this day they are the worst population of the district, rougher and less educated—though still rich. The Eastern portion of the district was poor and thin—yet it was almost wholly Whig.

EDWARD MUSGROVE, who built the mills, and resided there during the war, and long after, was from England, being one of the first settlers of the upper country. He had been bred to the law; was a man of education and fine abilities; was famous for his hospitality and benevolence. He was the surveyor and counsellor of law to all the surrounding country before the war, and in these departments was exceedingly useful. His personal appearance was remarkable, a little above (the ordinary size).

HOOK'S DEFEAT.—A pencil memorandum says: Tories and British, 1000; Americans, 260; that Lacey led 130, and Neil 130; that the horses of the Americans were hitched in a direct line from Williamson's house to Col. Bratton's and about as far beyond, apparently, as from Williamson's to Bratton's.

BATTLE OF MUSGROVE'S MILLS.—By Capt. P. M. Waters.

Williams and Shelby arrived at nightfall in the vicinity of the Tory camps, and took up their quarters in an old Indian field one mile from the river. Here they held a position till daybreak. They sent out a scout of some five or six men who went down to the river opposite the Tory camp. Having done this, they were returning by the same route, when on the top of the ridge, they (encountered) a Tory patrol of about the same number of men, as an engagement instantly followed, in which one of the enemy fell dead, two were wounded, and two escaped to the Tory camp. Two of the Americans were slightly wounded. This happened just before day in the early morning. This put the whole Tory camp in commotion, and the men were called to arms—their cavalry of a hundred men being eight miles below on patrol duty in the neighborhood of Major Dillard, near Jones' Ford. The British officers, Col. Cruger and Major Innis, called a council of war in the house of Edward Musgrove, in the presence of his family. Their headquarters were in one of the rooms of this house. Innis was for marching over the river and fighting at once. Cruger insisted that they should defer the attack till the men got their breakfast, and the cavalry had come up. Innis prevailed, and a movement was made across the river, leaving one hundred men in reserve in the camp.

Williams and Shelby, as soon as they were informed of this movement, fell back from their position in the Indian field and then the main body took position for battle, leaving Col. Inman and his command about two hundred yards below, in the rear between the Americans and the enemy. Inman opened fire upon the enemy as soon as he came in sight and in reach; the fire was returned, and Inman continued to fire retreating, till he passed the wings of the American line, the Tories advancing and firing, came at length, immediately between the American lines. Williams and Shelby ordered that not a gun should be fired till they were within a few yards, in full exposure to the American riflemen. At this point, just before the American fire was delivered, Inman wheeled to take his position in the center between the two wings, when a musket ball through the forehead laid him dead, near the root of a Spanish oak that stood a few paces above the point where the new road now leaves the old mill road, whose remains are still to be seen.

At the first fire of the Americans fearful execution was done, and the Tories fell back in disorder. In this Col. Cruger was shot through the back of the neck, and was ever after much stiffened. *Innis* was shot from his horse, and instantly ordered the British line to retreat and made a running fight retreating to the river; and as they passed the river, the Americans pressed them so close, as to kill many of them in the water. A rock not now visible, is said to have given an opportune resting place for some sixteen wounded men. Just as they crossed, the reserve men were prevented from giving any assistance from the fear of shooting their own men. It was at this point that the Americans retreated fearful of *Ferguson,* and having heard of the news of *Gates'* defeat.

Sixteen Tories are said to have been buried in one pit near the mouth of the creek. This spot has long since been defaced and lost. They were buried in a grave-yard just below *Musgrove's* house; several graves are still discernible on the spot where the Tories ·fell in such numbers at the first fire. The spot is a stone's throw below *George Gordon's* house, on the west side of the old road. Many were buried in the yard of Capt. *Philemon Waters,* who lives at present midway between the Ford and the battle-ground.

The table on which the dead were laid out, is still preserved in the family of Capt. *Philemon Waters,* grandson of *Edward Musgrove.* Half an hour after the battle, the cavalry having heard the firing, came rushing up to the camp. *Margaret Musgrove,* mother of Capt. *Waters,* and then 12 years old, says it was the grandest sight she ever saw as they came at full speed down the steep hill along which the old road ran to the east of the present house occupied by Dr. Bobo—their uniforms and rake (?) blades flashing in the sun just risen in full splendor above the lofty hill under which her father's house stood. They dashed up and the commanding officer asked what was the matter. The account of the battle was given him in a few words, on which rising in his stirrups, and uttering several deep and loud imprecations, he commanded his men to cross the river. They dashed at full speed into the water, which *Margaret* told afterwards played in rainbows around their horses. The enemy, however, were far out of their reach, and they were left nothing but the melancholy duty of burying the dead, and conveying the wounded to the hospital at *Musgrove's.*

Williams and *Shelby* were forced to leave their wounded to the mercy of the Tories. They were few, however. *Mrs. Waters (Margaret Musgrove)* says that when the enemy crossed the river and began their attack on *Inman,* the reserve force that remained at the camp, got on top of the house, and watched the progress of the battle as long as they remained in sight. They saw *Inman* deliver a fire and retreat, and continue to retreat, taking this to be the whole American force, and that they were therefore routed, they threw up their hats and shouted till the hill rang again. At length the battle had gone out of sight, when suddenly a tremendous roar (volley) of shot came booming back to the river. A deathly paleness covered their faces; some fifty of them who were paroled British prisoners doing duty contrary to the laws of war, and their countenances fell—the shouting ceased, and the declaration went around as soon as the returning fire of the British was heard: "We are beat—out men are retreating." And long before the Tories recrossed the river before the Americans, these men had seized their knap-sacks and scampered towards Ninety Six. She says the noise made by the retreating Tories and British as they ran (through) the woods, and over the hills to the river, was most awful, and taken with the vast volumes of smoke that rose high above the scene, it formed a terrific sight, well calculated to make a lasting impression upon the mind of a young girl.

Half way from the first attack where *Inman* fell, the Tories ceased to fight altogether—the retreat had become a rout—and now with wreckless speed they hastened to the ford through which they rushed with wild fury, the pursuing Americans still driving them with the sword and rifle.

GEN. PICKENS.—Andrew Shellito's Tradition.—

After the surrender of Charleston, the people, however, being still in the old Pickens Block House for fear of the Indians, they fell short of corn, when the following men were sent with wagons to Coroneaco Creek, famous for its corn, to get a supply—*Hugh Porter* (father of Alexander Porter), once a pastor of Cedar Springs Church, now in Ohio) *Jared Liddle, Enos Crawford, Andrew White, Matthew Thomson,*

James Beard, and one *Smith*—the last three lads—*Finley*, and one of the brothers of *Andrew Pickens*, (The names of his brothers were *John* and *Joseph*)—and yet others, names not recollected. They had crossed McCord's Creek early in the morning (and were to have been followed from the fort by a guard detailed for that purpose, commanded by one *Anderson*, who afterwards moved to Anderson District, and became a Colonel of militia, when his cowardice on this occasion showed him unworthy of any command), and when ascending the hill leading up to where West Croman now lives, they were attacked by a party of Tories under one *John Crawford*. They shot three of the Americans on the spot—*Enos Crawford, Hugh Porter* and one of *Pickens'* brothers. It may have been that Pickens was killed by the Indians after they reached the nation, which gave rise to the report that one of them was burnt. They took the rest of the party prisoners, and carried them North across the Saluda—for *James Beard* said afterwards, that if the guard under *Anderson* had pursued them the prisoners could have been retaken when crossing that river. *Anderson* did pursue them as far as Coronaco, and when crossing that creek he accidentally fell in, and regarding it as a bad omen, he turned back and gave up the pursuit. They took their prisoners beyond the Cherokee line, which then ran about two miles north of where Dr. Linch now lives, and near Trible's store, and gave them up to the Indians, who put to death in cold blood the most of them—among them my uncle, *Andrew White*, then only about seventeen. I know not the names of all who were thus killed, but it is certain he perished, and that only the three lads, *Beard, Smith* and *Thomson* ever returned. The report came back, and was always believed by many, that the Indians burnt their victims alive, but the lads testified that they were shot. They were put into a ring together to be shot, when the lads were spared by the intercession of the young squaws who had taken a fancy to them.

When my uncle saw that his fate was sealed, he said to *James Beard*, "Tell my brother *James* that I called to *Craw-*

ford for quarters, and he refused it." This message *Beard* faithfully delivered, and evil would have been the day for *Crawford* had he set his foot in that region again. *Andrew White* was shot, and his body left on the ground to rot.

JOHN CRAWFORD was never seen in Abbeville afterwards—he and many other villainous refugee Tories retired to St. Mary's, in Florida. My uncle and others went to St. Mary's in pursuit of him, but could never find him. He was then the richest man in this part of the country, owning a large body of land five miles below the village of Abbeville—son of *James Crawford*, who owned the stone plantation there. Crawford was loth to lose this fine property, and was afraid after the war to return—so sent his wife Peggy back to see the prospects—and when the Whig women of the neighborhood heard of her presence, they went in a body to the house where she was, at a sister's, and near relatives of the *Cunningham's*,—they drew Peggy by the heels from the house, took her out, tied her, and gave her a terrible whipping, each taking their turn. It was notorious in the community that she had conveyed to her husband the information about the wagons going to Coronaco for corn, as related. She returned to St. Mary's, and neither she nor her husband were ever heard of afterwards—his lands were sold by an attorney.

Another Mss.—a fragment, or apparently misplaced and separated from the connecting sheets—says:

DAVID MCCLURE, son of old *James*, lived on South Fork. David was a good Whig, and a pious man,—carried his Bible with him in all his campaigns of the Revolution.

ROBERT HANNAH, the elder of Duncan's, was the old surveyor of the settlement. He would occasionally take a wee bit too much. All the lands titles of the settlement being burnt up in their houses by the Tories, the Legislature granted them the privilege of a *resurvey* and a good title on that—*Hannah* did the surveying.

MUSGROVE'S MILLS BATTLE.—Another paper, apparently also by Capt. *Waters* (grandson of Edward Musgrove) already quoted—as Margaret Musgrove is also cited—says: That among the American wounded left at Musgrove's was one named Miller—shoe through the body, and believed to be mortal, and had to draw a silk handkerchief through his body to cleanse the wound; his parents were from the lower part of Laurens, and got a physician, old Dr. Ross, to attend to him, though it is believed the British surgeons were quite attentive. He recovered.

Among the wounded, besides Col. Cruger, was Col. Innis —he was shot from his horse early in the action; it is not related whether he ever recovered.

EDWARD MUSGROVE: (Found the remainder of the sketch of him, the first part of which already given, viz.:

"A little above the medium height, slender, venerably gray even at 30, and a magnificent head. He was in character, of great firmness and decision. As counsellor and magistrate, he married a great number of the old settlers. He bore the title of Major with all the old settlers. He died in the year 1792, in his 76th year, and was buried in the little grave-yard just behind the site of his house at the mill. He was three times married, and it was his third wife who was alive when the battle of the mills was fought—her name was *Nancy Crosby*, from near the Fish Dam Ford of Broad River. She survived till 1824, to a very advanced age—the grandmother of Capt. P. M. *Waters and* Dr. E. M. Bobo.

MARGARET, the oldest of her children was 21 at the time of the battle, and *Nancy, Hannah, Leah, Rachel*, and *Lenny* (*Lena?*) and William, were her children. Edward *Musgrove's* second wife was a Miss *Fincher*—the mother of *Susan*, and *Mary*, the renowned heroine of *Horse-Shoe Robinson*. Mary Musgrove was not only a woman of rare beauty, but of extraordinary mind and energy. Maj. Musgrove had more negroes than any one else in all that region, and was regarded very wealthy.

BEAKS MUSGROVE was a son by his first wife. *Paddy Carr* once hunting for *Beaks,* caught him in his father's house at the mill. He had come in to change his clothing, and get some refreshment; *Mary* was preparing him a meal; he had leaned his sword against the door lintel. *Paddy* came suddenly upon him, and took him before he could think of escape. *Paddy* said: "Are you Beaks Musgrove?" "I am, sir." "You are the man, sir, I have long sought." *Mary* seeing the drawn sword of her brother in *Carr's* hand, said: "Are you Paddy Carr?" I am *Mary Musgrove*, Mr. Carr; and you must not kill my brother," at the same time throwing herself between them. An interview now took place between *Carr* and *Musgrove*. *Carr* was struck with his manly beauty, and said: "*Musgrove,* you look like a man that would fight." "Yes, said *Musgrove,* "there are circumstances under which I would fight." "If I had come upon you alone," said *Carr,* "in possession of your arms, would you have fought me?" "Yes, sword in hand." *Carr* was so taken with *Musgrove* that he proposed to him to become a member of his scout and go with him on the spot, and swear never to bear arms against the American cause. His men had been stationed in the cedars some distance from the house, and had by this time come up to the scene. *Mary* seeing her brother disposed to accede to *Carr's* proposition, her fears for his safety being still awake, challenged *Carr* for his motives. "Mr. Carr," she said, "you do not design to persuade my brother to leave me, and then, when the presence of his sisters is no longer a restraint, butcher him in cold blood; pledge me, sir, that such is not your design." "I'll swear it," said *Carr*. *Musgrove* joined his party, continued some time with them, still gaining upon the confidence of *Carr;* but how long the native baseness of his heart permitted him to sustain his new character, is not recorded; it has been rumored, however, that he never afterwards bore arms against his country. Soon after, or about the close of the war, he left the country and never returned. He left a son who is now living, a Baptist preacher, who has displayed much of the eccentricity and acuteness of Lorenzo Dow.

MUSGROVE'S MILLS BATTLE.—It is further added in this narrative of Capt. Waters: "The next day after the battle, every woman and child of the surrounding country that was able to leave their homes, was on the spot—some for plunder, some for curiosity, and a few for a very different purpose. The surrounding country was chiefly Tory, and the few Whigs who belonged to it were out with *Sumter* or some other Whig leader. A few, therefore, of the Whig families came to examine the dead bodies, to see if any of their friends and relatives had fallen among the dead. The sisters of the Farrows were there (related to Col. *Philemon Waters*); they had not heard for some time from their brothers, and knew that it was more than probable, that some, if not all, had followed Col. *Williams* to the fight. Miss *Mary* Farrow, *Sarah* and *Jane*, looked at the dead, turning over or examining their faces. There were at least a hundred men, women and children on the spot the next day, and yet not one ever said anything afterwards of a brush breast-work that had been thrown up (by the Americans.)

MARY MUSGROVE.—The following incident occurred at her death: She requested that Mary Farrow, Mary Puckett, *Sarah Musgrove,* and a Miss *George*, should be her pall-bearers. The body being very light, they bore it to the grave on silk handkerchiefs. Just as they were lowering it into the grave, a kind-hearted old lady present, but who was the wife of a Tory, came forward to assist, when a member of the family interposed and prevented it. *Mary* had been a devoted Whig in principle.

Thomas, John, Samuel and *Landon Farrow,* bachelor brothers lived on the Cedar Shoal, four miles above (Musgrove's) Mill, and between Musgrove's and Heads Ford, who were from Virginia, and nephews of Col. *Philemon Waters*. No more stanch Whigs, or braver men drew sword for the good cause than these brothers. *Rosa* was their mother's name. The Farrows were at King's Mopntain; Sanmuel and Thomas were much scarred by their wounds in the war.

Capt. *Robbin Hannah* lived on the Musgrove's road, 3 miles south of the mill, on Hannah Hill.—He was a true and active Whig. *Golden Finsley* lived on the Musgrove road, 4 miles above (on the river; he was an intrepid Whig, and was at King's Mountain, Blackstock's and other important actions.

(The following narrative, I think taken by Dr. *Logan*, is not indicated who derived from,—perhaps "Col. Wallis" or *Wallace,* of York:—L. C. D.)

THE CARROLLS, HENDERSONS AND HATCHFORDS. COL. WALLACE. (David?)

The Carrolls settled first on Allison's Creek. There were three brothers who took a part in the Revolution,—*Thomas, John* and *Joseph*. Old *Joseph Carroll* was the father. They came from Pennsylvania. *John* and *Thomas* C. afterwards lived near Ebenezer. There were three families connected who came the same time from Pennsylvania, and settled on Fishing and Allison's Creeks, York Dist.,—they were the *Hatchfords, Carrolls* and *Hendersons*. They were all true Whigs, and staunch Presbyterians; it is said that these families contributed 16 strong men to the cause of Liberty, all of whom saw active service, and came off without a scratch, except John Hatchford, who was shot at Hanging Rock. He was however, fortunate enough to recover.

Capt. *John Moffett* lived up on the head of Bullock's Creek.

Col. *Andrew Lowe*, Col. *Wm. Hill* and Col. *Wm. Bratton* were the leading men of Eastern York in the Revolution.

When *Sumter* was elected by the militia Brigadier-General, his competitors were Cols. *Bratton* and *Hill*.

Col. *Neal,* Sr. was a prominent man also in York. Col. *Neal,* Jr. his son, was killed at *Rocky Mount*. He is supposed to have been a Captain on the Snow campaign. They lived on Crowder's Creek, in northeastern York, and were Pennsylvanians.

After the fall of Charleston, *Sumter* kept the field, and retired to N. Carolina, with a few partisan followers. The *Catawbas,* some 200, were also with him. Old *Robert Wilson,* who lived near the Lockhart Shoals, on Broad river, Chester, and a true patriot, also joined *Sumter* (15th June, 1780.) He says that when he arrived in the camp, the (Catawba) Indians had put a strange feature upon the ground by stretching cowhides between the trees, for fear of being attacked by cavalry—they had a great fear of cavalry—(hides doubtless of beeves killed in camp—and the Indians' fear inspired by the recent attack of Tarleton in that region on *Buford.*—L. C. D.)

The circumstances of *Wilson's* joining the camp were these. He had been made a prisoner at the fall of Charleston, and sent on parole Haddell's Point to nurse the sick; watching his opportunity, he soon after escaped, and traveling by nights through swamps and thickets arrived safely at his father's house in Chester. A few days after, Col. *Mayfield* sent out a detachment of Tories to murder *Joseph Robinson* and other Whigs of that vicinity; and calling at his father's, made young Wilson a prisoner a second time. *Wilson* knew if he was ever discovered, his fate was sealed, and immediately proposed to join the Royal cause on the condition that he would be allowed to go into the cavalry service: he was tired of the infantry. His proposition was as readily accepted; and they offered to give him a horse and other accoutrements, which he declined, saying that he had both arms and a good horse, and that he would meet them next morning by 8 o'clock at the cross-roads. When telling it afterwards, he used the significant phrase: "If a man can spin, he should learn to turn." *Sale Coffee,* who commanded the Tory scout, suddenly remarked now that they were forgetting orders, and that they should hurry on to find *Roberson,* and obey orders.

"Kill Joe Roberson!' exclaimed *Wilson* with the utmost composure, "well, you'll have to ride fast to do that; it is now nearly sundown, and he lives a good bit of a way from here." Now, *Roberson's* house was nearly in sight. The *ruse* took; the Tories at last concluded to wait till next day to obey orders on *Roberson*. *Wilson* slipt down to *Roberson's*, apprising him of his danger, and mounting their horses, rode all night and joined *Sumter* by the hour he was to have met the Tories the same morning. *Wilson* was a man of great intelligence, and an excellent citizen, a true Whig, and an elder in the Harmony Church.

Captain *James Reid,* of the same region, was meanly murdered in the yard of a treacherous Tory neighbor, who calling him as he was passing from his home back to (Sumter's) camp, as a friend, promising to go with him to *Sumter's* camp, shot him dead in cold blood. Capt. Reid had gone to see his wife, who was near her confinement, and to get some clean clothing.

It is remarkable that *Robert Wilson and* many of his gallant and patriotic associates arrived at advanced ages. *Robt. Wilson* died 14th Aug., 1850, some 93; Col. *Wm. Hillhouse* was still living at last accounts in Mississippi; *Joseph Jameson*, died in 1852, over 90; *Robert Cowley* died in 1848 or 49, over 90; *Henry Ray* died 88 years old.

Maj. *Meek*, Capt. John *Hood* and several other Whig partisans succeeded in ridding the country of the notorious *Mayfield* of Union, whose house was the rallying point for the Tories. He was a muscular bully of the times, and kept also a grocery—he was disposed of in the following manner. They dressed themselves in British uniform, and approached the house dragging *Meek along* with them as a Whig prisoner. Mayfield knew none of them, and was disposed to believe them to be what they seemed; but before getting quite into their hands, he suspected something, and turned to fly. *Hood* exclaimed: "You may run, sir, but I have something here to overtake you," and levelling his rifle shot him dead. The ball passed through his head. *Meek* was father-in-law of Mr. *John S. Moore,* of York.

Meek and Hood went side by side through all the privations and dangers of the Revolution, and escaped without a wound. They were at Briar Creek, Rocky Mount, Hanging Rock, Sumter's defeat at Fishing creek, Fish Dam Ford, Blackstock's, Biggin Church and Entaw Springs. At Entaw Hood's hunting shirt was pierced with seven bullets.

FISHING CREEK SURPRISE.—At Fishing Creek Hood lost his gun and horse, and escaped on foot. The camp was totally unprepared for an attack—some of the men were asleep—some bathing in the creek—some playing cards—some cooking. *Sumter* was asleep in a brush tent: and when wakened up by his men on the approach of the enemy, he rose up, rubbed his eyes, took in at glance the situation, and exclaimed, "Let every man take care of himself." *Wilson* says that he sprung upon his horse, and jerked the bridle from the limb to which it was hitched, and made his escape, with a couple of British troopers close at his heels, across the old Nation Ford.

Hood was an Irishman, a millwright. He did good service after the war in ridding the country of the race of horse-thieves that then infested it. He lived on Clarke's Ford. He died about forty years ago (prior probably to about 1858, which would indicate about 1818—L. C. D.) in the Sequatchee Valley of Tennessee. His widow, *Mary Hood,* removed to Texas, Titus County, and died there in 1857. Hood, towards the close of the war, in the reckless license of the times, shot a Tory while sitting in his wife's lap.

Major *Edward Meek's* descendants have long been among the most useful and respectable citizens of York District. He lies in Bersheba church grave-yard.

SUMTER'S GATHERING AT HAGLER'S BRANCH.—Wilson and Robeson who joined *Sumter* as above related, found him at *Hagler's Branch,* and a few days after at this place, they elected Col. Sumter Brigadier-General, and their other officers.

This was June 15th, 1780. This was the first organization of the militia after the fall of Charleston. They elected at this time, *Andrew Neal* Colonel; *John McCool*, Captain; *James Reid*, Captain; and *Robert Wilson* and *Wm. Hillhouse* were elected Lieutenant and Ensign of *McCool's* Company.

Sumter was chosen over his competitors (Cols. *Bratton* and *Hill*) chiefly on account of his having served in the S. C. Continental line previously. He had with him here besides the *Catawbas,* some two or three hundred men, refugees chiefly from S. C. generally mounted and armed with rifles. They soon after moved down to *Clem's Branch* of Steel Creek (first written "Sugar Creek"—but "Sugar" erased, and "Steel" substituted. L. C. D.), where the grazing was better for their horses. This gave the Whigs confidence, and they flocked in considerable numbers to *Sumter's camp*, which soon made him strong enough to face the enemy.

Near this bend is the Horse Shoe Bend in Sugar Creek, where lived in the Revolution Robertson, who is the hero of *Horse Shoe Robertson.*

Just before *Sumter* removed from *Hagler's Branch*, he was joined by Capt. *James Jamieson*, from *Bullock's* Creek, with eleven men. The circumstances of his coming were these: There came to Bullock's Creek a detachment (rather a flying party of fugitives—L. C. D.) of Whigs, some 500 men, who encamped near the church. The next morning they called a council of war in the church to deliberate what should be done, and invited young *Jamieson* to take part in the council; but he refused to sit with them, declaring that it was not a council of war they were to hold, but a council of flight. The result was as he expected—they resolving that the cause was hopeless, and advised every man to shift for himself. *Jamieson* then stepped forward and said: "There are men who are contending for Liberty, and all who join me in a continuation to the last for Liberty, let them meet me tomorrow morning at sun-rise, and retreat to the North till we meet with a force sufficiently strong to enable us to make a stand." Eleven men met him, and they joined Sumter as related. They did not hear of Sumter's stand at Hagler's till they had crossed the Catawba river. Jamison was a young man of such intrepidity and integrity of character, as to have won at an early age the confidence of all who knew him. He was remarkable for his personal appearance, and uncompromising firmness in any cause he deemed a just one. He had been educated under the teachings of Rev. Dr. Alexander.

Sumter now crossed the old Nation Ford and attacked the enemy at *Rocky Mount,* July 30, 1780. Here Col. *Andrew* Neal fell, shot through the shoulders. Sumter withdrew: and on the 6th day of August following the enemy at *Hanging Rock,* in Lancaster. Capt. *Neel* (Col. McClure? L. C. D.) was shot through the haunch—the ball entered one of the hips and came out on the opposite side of the abdomen. He was here under either *Hill* or *Lacey.* His command was to pass up the valley of Hanging Rock Creek, to ascend the bluff opposite the enemy's encampment, which was both steep and rugged. He was the first to gain the top of the bluff, and turning around at that point, said to his men, "Come on, my brave fellows," when he received a shot from a sentinel, and fell, it was thought mortally wounded. "Fight on, my brave boys: liberty will do me no good, but will yet live." They first encountered Bryan's Tories, mostly from North Carolina, which they soon cut to pieces and drove from the field, and took their camp—three times did this occur—first in and out of the enemy's camp, till they at last drove them from the field (*Jamieson's* and *Robert Wilson's* testimony.) The wounded were sent to Charlotte after the battle, and here after lingering in a tedious sickness *Jamieson,* who was wounded at Hanging Rock, finally recovered and returned home. Shortly after, he was captured by a scout from *Cornwallis' army,* and being accused to his Lordship as one of the worst of rebels, with the wish that he should be hung at once. *Cornwallis* ordered him to be brought before him, that he might interrogate him, and ended by offering inducements to join the British army, which he indignantly refused. Cornwallis then asked him what he had to answer for killing the King's troops. "If ever I killed any of the King's men, it was in battle, in the defense of my country, except on one occasion when I killed an Indian. I know that I killed that King's man, because we were alone, in a personal conflict." On this he was dismissed without further molestation. Cornwallis carried him with him to Charlotte; on the route, from exposure, his wound broke out afresh, and came near destroying his life. He was at Charlotte, when Ferguson was routed at King's Mountain. He noticed through the (window?) that there was some excitement in the camp, produced by the arrival of despatches that told of his danger. About 11 o'clock at night, a man came rushing up to the camp, and was instantly led (into) the markee; and from the effect produced by his narration he conjectured some British force had met a discomfiture. Presently another came running up who proclaimed that *Ferguson* had been defeated and killed, and he alone had escaped. *Jamieson* lying on his back, unable to rise, perhaps involuntarily exclaimed, "Well, thank God for that." Soon after that he was released on parole. He saw no more service during the war. This was Jan., 1781. He died in 1839, and lies at Bullock's Creek.

Capt. Robert Wilson was half brother of Hon. John Wilson, who was for a long time a member of Congress from the Ninety Six District, and succeeded by Hon. Warren R. Davis. His widow still lives near Blairsville, S. C., and enjoys a pension for the services of her husband.

Capt. Peter Clinton lived on the Catawba, in the Bethel Congregation; his place is still owned by his son, Joseph Clinton. He was, in 1775, a Captain under Col. Neel and commanded a company on the Snow campaign under him (Gen. Richardson's command of six regiments—three of S. C. and three of N. C.). He was also with the same Colonel (Neel) under Gen. Williamson in the Indian campaign of 1776. He next served under Col. Neel with Williamson in the expedition into Georgia that resulted in the battle of Brier Creek. He returned safely home from this battle to the bosom of his family, but soon after sickened and died, in 1779, leaving a wife and two children. Clinton was a man of great promise. He lies buried at Bethel, of which he was a member.

Col. Ben Roebuck lived on Tyger, in Spartanburg District. Capt. George Roebuck, a younger brother of the Colonel, lived near by him. Col. Roebuck never married. He was a most intrepid soldier. He served over two years as Colonel and Lieut. Colonel of the 1st Spartanburg regiment. This regimnt is said to have been the finest in the service. It is apparent from the records of the State, Capt. Major Parsons served 800 days in this regiment; he lived above Spartanburg C. H. Col. Tom Farrow belonged to Roebuck's regiment; he first volunteered as a private in Capt. Sanders' company, and was at the battle of Cross Creek; after this he came to S. C., and on the 20th June, 1776, volunteered in Capt. Ben Kilgore's company,—Col. James Williams—and Gen. Williamson. Under these officers he served through the Indian campaign of 1776; Nov., 1778, he was commissioned Lieut. under Capt. John Ford, in Col. John Thomas, Sr's regiment. At this time Roebuck was Major in that regiment—White (Lieut.) Colonel. He (Farrow) was taken prisoner at the fall of Charleston, and was paroled by Col. Cruger. He died in 1842. He was the father of Col. Patillo Farrow, who was several years representative in Congress from Spartanburg.

Capt. Wm. Smith raised a company of Light Dragoons, in Col. John Thomas regiment, Sumter's Brigade, of State Troops—41 officers and privates in the company. Maj. Wm. Smith died in 1837; he was Judge of ordinary for Spartanburg District. He was in Congress for the Spartanburg Congressional District. He was the father of Dr. J. Winn Smith, Isaac Smith, Ralph Smith, Wm. Eliphas Smith and E. P. Smith.

The State troops of South Carolina were raised by a resolution of the State Legislature, April, 1781, for a period of ten months, and every private was promised a grown negro, besides his bounty for that much service—this service closed in

April, 1782. The negroes were confiscated property of the Tories. The property of those was confiscated only, who had rendered themselves particularly obnoxious. The soldiers of the State troops did receive their pay in this manner as far as the negroes would go, and the rest were paid by indents in money. A grown negro was estimated at 400 dollars (coin, doubtless—L. C. D.) : one above 40, or under 12 was estimated, and so marked on the payrolls as a half negro. This was Sumter's Brigade, with Cols. Hampton, Myddelton, John Thomas, Wm. Hill and Sam Hammond.

Maj. Frank Ross lived on Turkey Creek, near York village —he was a Pennsylvanian, and one of the first settlers of that district. He was a man of bright talents, and of such integrity that all the country placed in his judgment and councils the most implicit confidence. He was a patriot at the very first movement of the Revolution—passed through the Indian campaign of 1776 under Col. Neel, being a captain. He is honorably mentioned in Ferris' book. He was killed by a wounded Indian in some skirmish with the Cherokees about the year 1779 or '80, and fell universally regretted.

Capt. John Miller was his brother-in-law, and was also distinguished as a Revolutionary soldier—he fell at Hanging Rock—received a mortal wound through the ankle, and died at Charlotte, where his body still lies. Capt. James Martin was a nephew of Maj. Ross and an active patriot from the first of the war. Capt. Miller lived on the place now owned on Turkey Creek, by Judge Ross, his grandson. Martin also lived on Turkey Creek: he was a captain as early as 1779, and served at Briar Creek—Wm. Wallace was his first Lieutenant. He served after the war ten years in the Legislature, and was member of the Convention that adopted the Constitution. At Briar Creek Wm. Wallace was unable to swim, and was carried over the river by his brother, Leroy Joseph Wallace, while Wm. carried the guns: they got safe over, but lost one of the guns. There were many drowned in the river in this route. Capt. Martin told of a poor fellow whom he endeavored to save, being unable to swim. He told him to put his hands on his hips and he would carry him over; he set out, when the man jumped upon his back and they both sank—he returned to the bank and tried it with him again, with the same result, when he (Martin) plunged in and saved himself alone, leaving him on the bank to his fate—the British were already running along the bank, shooting those who were struggling in the river.

Capt. Hugh Bratton, cousin of Col. Wm. Bratton, was also an active Whig.

HOOK'S DEFEAT.—When the Whigs approached at Hauk's defeat, they supposed they would find him about White's Mills, on Big Fishing Creek: two of them got separated from the company (of Whigs) at that point, and wandered off to old John Gill's, where lived Mary Gill, his daughter, who afterwards became the wife of Capt. John Mills. Mary undertook to pilot them through the forest to the main road; the night was dark and the way intricate—she tied a white handkerchief around her neck and walked before them two miles to the road, and then bidding them God speed, returned alone. The men mistook the water in the pond for the camp of Hauk. Mary Gill was then interested for Mills.

Cornwallis encamped on Turkey Creek at Wm. and John Hillhouse's; he also encamped on the same at the Quin road (or Twin road) and Howell's Ferry—Wm. Carr then lived there; it is now owned by Wm. Berry.

(End of this narrative.—L. C. D.)

BLACKSTOCK'S.—Col. I. S. Sims to Dr. Logan, Sept. 4, 1858.

Old Major Otterson told me that at Blackstock's Sumter had his horses fastened under a hill in his rear, and formed his line of battle in the protection of a dwelling house and some out-houses, and a fence in their front; that Tarleton let down the fence opposite them and marched up to them in the open field. Sumter's orders were not to fire till the enemy were within sixty yards of them. The battle continued in this position, until Tarleton withdrew his force; and at the same time Sumter mounted his men and each party made for the ford on Tyger River—Sumter led his men, in single file, by a small path in the woods; all of a sudden the British formed on the big road, and fired at them, when Sumter was wounded in the shoulder, and a man by the name of Brown, the next man to Sumter was killed.

COWPENS.—Col. Sims adds:

Old Mr. Adam Gouldelock, father of Mrs. Sallie Murray, and several grown children at the time of these events, lived at the fork of the roads, two miles North of Grindal's Shoals, the place where Mrs. Nancy Dawkins, widow of the late Gen. E. Dawkins, now lives. Mr. Murray had been sent by a British officer, with a paper of protection to her sister, Mrs. Sapold, whose husband was in the British service and whose family lived near the Cowpens. She heard a great part of the battle and got home to Adam Gouldelock's before Col. Washington arrived there in pursuit of Tarleton, who had taken the old man Gouldelock along with him to pilot him to the Hamilton's Ford on Broad river, about two miles above the mouth of Pacolet. She was sitting in their piazza when Col. Washington rode up. Some inquiries were made and answers given, when the old lady said to him, "You will not attempt to go any further, so late as it is." He replied, "No, madam, this is as far as I expected to pursue when I started; but if I desired to do so, my horse could not carry me, for look there"—pointing his sword to a severe wound in his horse's shulder. He then engaged the family to nurse and take care of several wounded prisoners that he had with him, and returned with his troops. This is old Mrs. Murray's account."

Refers to pension declaration of Nicholas Curry, an honest old soldier of the Upper part of this District (Union), a copy of which would be worth having.

Gen. Wm. Henderson—to his brother, Capt. John Henderson, Granville County, N. C.

Gen Henderson writes, July 1st, 1782, Congaree:

"Every circumstance indicates the enemy leaving Charleston in about a fortnight or three weeks. See the militia within eighty miles of town are called down, and one-half above that (or beyond this distance—L. C. D.) My Brigade is now marching down to be prepared for any event. The enemy will certainly leave this country, or collect the force from Savannah, which they have evacuated, and from St. Augustine, and endeavor to keep a strong garrison."

Gen. Henderson, also to his brother John—Charleston, 10th March, 1784:

"I have been here attending the Asesmbly five weeks. * * * If I were to give you a detail of all the business before the House, it would take a quire of paper. I will only mention the tax bill, which I expect will scare you: two and a half dollars per head on all negroes; one per cent. on the value of all the lands in this State. This is all the tax that will affect the upper part of the country. The demands for money were so great, that we were obliged to lay this tax. It is certainly the most equal that can be laid, because the rich must pay the chief of the same. We have classed all the lands in the State. The first quality in your parts is valued at eight shillings per acre, and so down to one shilling. The first quality down here at six pounds, and down to five shillings. These are the principal heads of the tax act. The taxes are to be received in the interest of indents, so that I hope the people will not be obliged to pay much money. Those that have not received their indents, are to have certificates of the amount of their accounts, and settle by that.

To Capt. John Henderson, Packolate."

Gen. Robert Irwin's Birth.—Among the papers of Capt. John Irwin, is the following list of births of the children of his father, Wm. Irwin, viz.:

1. Alexander Irwin, born December, 1723.
2. Ann Irwin, born 1726.
3. Francis Irwin, born March 30, 1731.
4. Mary Irwin, born May 2, 1732.
5. John Irwin, born Feb. 19, 1735.
6. Margaret Irwin, born Aug. 10, 1736.
7. Wm. Irwin, born Feb. 22, 1738.
8. Robert Irwin, born Aug. 26, 1740.
9. Elizabeth Irwin, born April 23, 1742.
10. A child, died a few days after—April 21, (1743).
11. Sarah Irwin, born July 4, 1744.
12. James Irwin, born Aug. 19, 1745.
13. Samuel Irwin, born April 11, 1747.

GEN. ANDREW PICKENS.—Hon. F. W. Pickens writes to (Chas. H. Allen, Abbeville, S. C.)

EDGEWOOD, 26th March, 1848.

Dear Sir:—On my return home I found yours inquiring when the Block House near Abbeville, was built—and by whom? And you also inquire when my grandfather left Abbeville District, and how long he resided in it?

"Gen. Pickens built the Block House himself, about the year 1768. In 1761, the settlement on Long Cane was nearly exterminated by the terrible massacre of the Indians, and you will find the old tombstone near Long Cane Bridge, on the road leading from Calhoun's Mills and the old Hopewell Church to (sic) Hacolalor (?) Upon that you will see many of the names of those who were murdered, rudely inscribed. That old place that used to belong to Wm. Calhoun, South of Dr. Reed's (but formerly Col. Norris, my uncle) was amongst the first, if not the very first settlement, made in Abbeville District; and next to it was Patrick Calhoun's old place, where nearly all the Calhouns were born. After that massacre in 1761, Ezekiel Calhoun fled to the Waxhaws, the nearest white settlement, for protection.

My grandfather lived there, and then got acquainted with my grandmother, who was the daughter of Ezekiel Calhoun, and came back to the Calhoun's settlement with them, and married there. He then settled there in 1764, but in 1765 he moved to and settled at the place where the Block House is standing near Abbeville C. H. He built the Block House about 1768—perhaps 1767—and made it a resort for the neighbors to fly to in order to protect themselves from the Indians, he always taking command. He owned all the lands about the place where the present village stands, and I think sold to Maj. Hamilton, who was also a gallant soldier of the Revolution.

Maj. Alston must have the papers and deeds, which will show when he sold, and left for Hoepwell in Pendleton. But my notes indicate that he left Abbeville in the year 1787—if so, he resided in Abbeville from the first of 1764 to 1787, or 23 years.

In 1782 he raised and commanded 500 men, and made for them short cutlasses from the common blacksmith's shops of the country, and overrun and conquered the Cherokee nation in six weeks. They were then a very powerful people, but were so thoroughly conquered by the terrible slaughter in this new mode of warfare (but few firearms were used) that they sued for peace, and were afterwards our allies. He formed with them the treaty of Hopewell, 1785, November, by which Anderson, Pickens and Greenville were obtained from them, or at least a portion of Greenville. The State gave him the place where the treaty was held (I believe), and in 1787, he settled there on the banks of the Seneca river, about three miles from old Pendleton C. H. After he removed to Pendleton, he and Col. Cleveland, of Greenville, constituted a court, and tried all cases, and executed their own laws for all that country for several years, and kept it in complete subjection as Judge Thomas could inform (you).

The other parts he performed in the battles of Kettle Creek, Stono, Cowpens, Augusta, Ninety Six and Entaws, etc., etc., you know as they are recorded generally in history.

When he built the block-house the neighborhood was a great resort for Indians who brought their ginseng, pink root, deer and bear skins and beaver, in large quantities; and he owned afterwards a warehouse opposite Augusta, near where the bridge now rests in Hamburg, to which place he sent all these things obtained from the Indians. He also sent droves of beef cattle to Philadelphia from both Abbeville and from Pendleton afterwards.

During the war his house near the Block House was burned down by the Tories, and his family lived for weeks in the woods near Abbeville, fed by their own negroes secretly.

And when Greene retreated from Ninety Six at the approach of a stronger force from Charleston, and crossed Saluda on his way to N. C. and Va., apparently to abandon South Carolina, my grandfather's family came into his camp to retreat with the army and avoid the Tories, but he immediately sent them back to Shew, (as he says) his neighbors and countrymen that he did not intend to give up the country, but would return if he returned alone.

Soon afterwards the battle of Cowpens was fought, and Morgan did not wish to fight them, but my grandfather in the council of war held the night before, said that he would fight it with his command alone (being the largest portion) if for nothing else, but to show the people of So. Car. that he did not give up the State, even if the Continentals and regulars did leave the State. You will recollect they were then on a retreat under Morgan and Greene before Tarleton and Cornwallis, and soon after fought the battle of Guilford, C. H. These facts are confirmed by Col. Howard's notes, who commanded the regulars, and his son has them now.

I could give you many details but I have loaned my notes to Mr. Pickett, of Montgomery, Ala., who is preparing a history of that State and the Indians. He heard of my notes, and wrote to beg me to loan them. I did so with pleasure, as I am not at all ambitious of being an author.

In the last number of the Southern Review, January number, published in Charleston, you will see an article written by myself, on "The Growth and Consumption of Cotton." I think you will find in it some tables at least very useful to Southern men and slave holders.

In great haste, but very respectfully and truly,

F. W. PICKENS.

CALHOUN SETTLEMENT.—Hon. J. C. Calhoun writes Nov. 21, 1847, Fort Hill, to Chas. H. Allen:

"My father (Patrick Calhoun) with his three brothers and his sister with her husband arrived in this district (Abbeville), February, 1756, and settled in a group in what is now known as Calhoun's Settlement, at the fort of the two streams of that name. The names of his brothers were James, the oldest, Ezekiel, the next, William, the third, my father being the youngest. The sister had married Mr. Noble, and the late Governor Noble was her grandson. My father settled on the place owned recently by a son of my brother Patrick, where a monument is raised to his memory. The elder brother settled on a place afterwards owned by my brother James, and now owned by Mrs. Parker. Ezekiel settled on the place on which she resides. William in the fork of Calhoun's Creek and Little River; and Mr. Noble in the fork of the two creeks of the name of Calhoun.

I am not certain who accompanied them, or who immediately followed them and settled in the neighborhood. But among their very early neighbors were Norris, who after the death of Ezekiel, married his widow: a family of the name of Mercer and one of the name of Houston, of which Squire Houston is a descendant, and probably can give you some information. Our family, however, were the pioneers, and my impression is, came alone. My father kept a journal of their emigration from Wythe County, as it is now called, in Virginia, but then the extreme limits to which the white population had advanced.

There were at the time they made their settlement but two others in the District: one at White Hall, on Hard Labor Creek, settled by Williamson, a Scotch trader, in 1754, and the other at Cambridge, then called Ninety Six, settled about the same time by a man of the name of Goudy, also a trader. The region composing the District was in a virgin state, new and beautiful, without underwood and all the fertile portions covered by a dense cane-brake, and hence the name of Long Cane. It had been recently got from the Cherokees, and the settlement was more than 16 or 17 miles from the boundary line between them and the whites. The region was full of deer and other game, and among them the buffalo.

Our family were driven from the back part of Virginia in consequence of Braddock's defeat in the old French war. The hostilities of the Indians (the war continuing) extended South; and in Feb., 1760, the Cherokees made a sudden inroad on Calhoun, and the other settlements, that had been formed subsequently. The inhabitants fled, but were overtaken by the Indians mounted on horseback. The entire number of whites, men, women and children, amounted to about 250, of which about 55 or 60 were capable of bearing arms; but the onset was so sudden that but few more than about 14, could get their arms out of the wagons in time to make resistance. They made a desperate struggle but with the loss, by being killed, of one-half the number; and among them James Calhoun, the oldest brother, who commanded the party. The killed altogether amounted to about 50, mostly women and children. The men who escaped, returned to bury the dead, pick up the stragglers, and recover what property might not be destroyed, and found 21 Indian warriors dead on the ground, and among them a principal chief. Those of the settlement who escaped, fled to Augusta. The battle was fought on the East side of

Long Cane, near where the old road from Calhoun's settlement to Charleston, called the Ridge Road, crossed it, at a place near to where Patterson's bridge crosses it. A tombstone erected by my father to the memory of his mother, who was among the killed (an old woman of seventy-six years of age) marks the spot.

KING'S MOUNTAIN BATTLE.—A writer on King's Mountain battle, "J. L. G.," in the Rutherford (N. C.) Enequirer, May 24, 1859, gives some traditions from which I select: "The first gun that was fired on the mountain that day killed one of Ferguson's sentinels. He was standing upon the road by which the Liberty men were approaching; and they had come within rifle shot of him before he perceived them. He fired his musket, and ran with all his speed toward the camp. One of the foremost of the mountaineers sprang from his horse, levelled his rifle, and fired at him as he ran. The ball struck him in the back of the head, and he fell and expired.

In the midst of the battle was an old man in whose bosom the fires of Liberty and patriotism so burned that infirmities of age were forgotten, and with nerves high strung with the hope of victory, and of Liberty for his beloved country, he had shouldered his rifle, shot-pouch, and powder-horn, and marched with the sons of Liberty to King's Mountain. While fighting gloriously for Liberty at the side of the mountain, this old man fell mortally wounded. A young man who was fighting by his side, and who had just shot away his last load of powder, said to him, "Old man, give me your powder-horn." The old man took off his powder-horn, and gave it to the young man, and died on the eve of victory. (The old man was William Robertson—he recovered.—L. C. D.)

On the top of the mountain the next morning, James Gray found an old acquaintance who had been wounded in the ankle, and unable to walk. He was not thought to have been one of those mean Tories who joined the King's Standard for the sake of being protected from rapine and murder. But he fought against his country because he thought it was right .to fight for the King. James Gray took a handkerchief from his pocket and bound up his broken ankle. He afterwards recovered from his wound, became a useful citizen to the country, and as long as he lived remained a strong friend to the man, who, though an enemy, showed kindness to him in the day of distress.

Some of the captured Tories were hung. Paddy Carr came up and looked at them as they were hanging on the trees, and said that he wished every tree in the woods bore such fruit as that.

When arrangements had been made for leaving the battle ground, the captured muskets were all stacked up on the top of the mountain, and when they were ready to march (there being no baggage wagons) orders were given for the prisoners to march in single file by the stack of muskets, and each one to shoulder and carry one. Old Shelby stood by with his sword drawn, to see that the order was strictly obeyed. One old fellow came toddling by, who was about to disobey the order, when Shelby ordered him to shoulder a musket. He said he was an old man, and not able to carry it. Shelby told him with a curse that he had brought one there, and he should carry one away, and at the same time gave him a rap across the shoulder with the flat side of his broad sword blade. The old fellow jumped at a musket, shouldered it, and marched away in quick time.

The prisoners were marched to Gilbert Town where was a Tory pen in which they had confined Whig prisoners—and a Tory woman there was asked what the Tories were going to do with them, replied, "We are going to hang all the Dn——d old rebels, and take their wives, scrape their tongues, and let them go." This same Tory woman now visited the Tory prisoners taken at King's Mountain, among whom was her husband, and with tears in her eyes asked James Gray, one of the guard, "What are you going to do with them poor fellows?" He retorted in her own language, to annoy and humble her, "We are gonig to hang all the d——d old Tories, and take their wives, scrape their tongues, and let them go." This confounded the Tory woman—the battle was against her and friends and she retreated.

SUMTER'S CAMP.—In one of the newspaper series, No. 19, of Judge O'Neall's Annals of Newberry, he says: "After the fall of Charleston, the Whigs scattered; some rendezvoused at Tuckasege Ford, on Catawba, under Sumter."

COL. LEROY HAMMOND.—Found references showing Col. LeRoy Hammond was in service in 1781,—as shown by records of Comptroller's office: and Col. Robuck in service from February, 1780, to 1782—certified by James A. Black.

And among Gen. Wm. Butler's pension papers, is evidence showing Col. L. Hammond was in service with his regiment in 1782.

GEN. PICKENS.—J. H. Marshall, of Anderson, C. H., writes Dr. Logan, May 13th, 1858, saying that last year he had commenced writing the Life of Gen. Pickens, and published some pieces on the subject, which attracted the attention of Col. F. W. Pickens, who wrote him some letters about his grandfather, one of which he has found and encloses—dated Edgewood, 4th Nov., 1847.

"I will mention a few facts not known or noticed much in general history. Gen. Pickens was actually chosen a Brigadier General in N. C. as successor to Gen. Davidson, and was a General at the same time from two States.

"After the great battle of the Cowpens, Morgan joined Greene and was pursued by Cornwallis, and the reason why Gen. Pickens was not at the battle of Guilford C. H., was that a few days before the militia under his command from Georgia and South Carolina, and from Rowan and Mecklenburg counties, N. C., were offended in the affair at "Whitsell's Mills;" and under the advice of Gov. Rutledge, who had arrived in camp, he marched them back into So. Carolina. It was on that occasion, too, he had been detached with Col. Lee in pursuit of Tarleton in North Carolina, who was rallying the Tories, and Gen. Pickens fell in with a body of 350 of them, Col. Piles' men, on Haw river, in the night, and the Tories cried, "God save the King," supposing it was Tarleton and his command, and while thus crying the watch-word, were cut entirely to pieces.

See National Portrait Gallery, in short life of Gen. Pickens. how he was so generously elected by Dooley and Clark to command in Georgia, after he crossed the Savannah river—preceding battle of Kettle Creek. I will give you a traditional anecdote connected with this battle. Col. Boyd who commanded the 700 Tories there, was from Newberry District, and Gen. Pickens knew him well. He was a brave, gallant, high toned man, devoted to his King and country. After Pickens had crossed, at Vienna, over Savannah river, Dooley and Clarke gracefully united with him and gave the command up; he pursued Boyd several days very closely. At last they came up with him on the slope of an open field on the East side of the creek. They had just killed some beeves, and were preparing breakfast, when Pickens instantly charged, and in the first charge Boyd was mortally wounded, and his men retreated over the creek in the cane and fought desperately. Afterwards Pickens came, as soon as he could, to Boyd, and said to him, "Boyd, I am pained to see you in such suffering, and in such a cause.'" Boyd instantly stopped him, and rose on his elbow and said, "Sir, I glory in the cause—I die for my King and country;" and then took off a brooch from his shirt, and handed it to Col. Pickens, and requested him to give it to his wife, and tell her he saw the last of him. He then died. Col. Pickens took the brooch afterwards, and delivered it to his wife, and told her "he died like a man." She was a large, masculine woman, and instantly turned on her heel, and exclaimed, "It was a lie—no d——d rebel had ever killed her husband."

THE COWPENS.—There are two incidents connected with the Cowpens I desire to state to you, which you can use by way of amusing and interesting the public at your leisure. Col. James Jackson, of Georgia, was his aid at the Cowpens, and actually received the sword of the Major of that battalion that surrendered on that day to Gen. Pickens and the militia. This battallion was the 1st of the 71st British regiment; and together with two Light Infantry companies were amongst the first of the British army selected for Tarleton and his rapid moves. These did not surrender to the regulars, but actually surrendered to South Carolina militia, and to a S. C. officer, Gen. Pickens, as you will see by what I enclose, and which I wish you to return. This was a remarkable fact, and I could give you the reason, but have no space now, and it involves others; but Gov. Swain, of N. C., is now preparing a history under the authority of N. C., of those times, and he will bring it out, and you will see how great the credit was when the real cause is known.

The other incident relates to his body servant, Old Dick. He was a faithful African, and had followed him through the Indian wars as well as the British, and actually fought by his side; and my father told me that Gen. Pickens, his father, often said Old Dick was as brave a man as ever faced battle. At the Cowpens the victory was complete, and the British soldiers were well dressed and supplied, while the Americans, particularly the militia, were very badly off for common clothes, and shoes even. After the battle was over, Dick was walking about the field, to see what was to be done. He came across a young British officer elegantly dressed, with fine fair top boots on, and badly wounded, with his head leaning on the root of a tree; and Dick stood up by him and placed his foot and knee out in the attitude to draw his boots, and the officer said to him, "Surely, my boy, you will not take them before I die." Dick—"Looked mighty nice, and Massa need 'em too bad." The officer then said, "I am so thirsty; bring me a little water before I die, and then take the boots." Dick went and filled his own hat with water and brought it, and the officer drank freely, and did die; Dick brought the boots to the tent of Gen. Pickens, and told it to all around.

On another occasion Dick swam Broad river twice one cold night, in the dead of winter, to get to the camp of his master—the first time he swam, he got into a camp of the enemy by mistake, and the second time he reached his master. He was with Gen. Pickens through the war.

When the Tories burnt Gen. Pickens' house, near the Block House, (at a time when he was off in the army) and drove the family to seek shelter and protection in the woods, for days, Dick and other servants furnished them with supplies, and nursed them, some of the children actually having small-pox, and one of the sons died with it.

Gen. Pickens always allowed Dick to the day of his death every privilege. He ever wore a long knife in a leather sheath, and belt by his side; and not even Gen. Pickens' sons were permitted to rebuke or cross Dick, and he said what he pleased. Gen. Pickens was the only man Dick always treated with profound deference.

RING FIGHT.—Perhaps you have never seen anything of Gen. Pickens' great "Ring Fight"—see Garden's Anecdotes of the Revolution, (Vol. 3, new edition, p. 78-9). It took place in 1779, (really Aug. 12, 1776 L. C. D.) At the very place where he afterwards settled in the latter part of his life and died, "Tamoosee," about twenty-two miles above old Pendleton village. He was with 25 men on a party of discovery, looking for the position of Indians, about two miles from the main force he had left under Col. Anderson; and suddenly, in the edge of an Indian field, they discovered the Indians rising in a circle around them. There was a half-breed by his side, a friendly man, named Cornels, who understood Indian well. The Indians paused, and Cornels said they passed the order around their ranks, to swing their rifles in the left hand, and tomahawk them as they (the whites) were but a "handful," and the rest "could not bear the guns." There were only 25 whites, and about 185 warriors. They formed the circle complete, and Col. Pickens immediately formed a countercircle, facing onwards to receive them, giving the order distinctly,

"Let every man sell his life as dear as possible, and no man fire till he can see the whites of their eyes." So they came advancing on foot to their prey, and the 25 drew and fired, and each man killed his man; and they were so astonished and confused that they fell into confusion and before they could recover, the whites had loaded again, and again each man brought his man. In the meantime some of the savages had also fired, and Cornels, the half-breed was shot down and Col. Pickens' rifle choaked, so he couldn't get it off, and he took up Cornels' immediately, and fired right on! They kept it up for 5 rounds, until some 83 of the Indians fell dead and wounded, and every white man was covered literally with blood and smoke—but Cornels was the only man actually killed on their side.

By this Capt. Joseph Pickens, a younger brother of Col. Pickens, heard the firing at the camp, and rushed out with some men, hastily picked up, to the help of his brother (although some said it was the cracking of the cane on fire). The Indians were beaten back, and about to break up, terrified by their dreadful slaughter, just as Capt. Pickens reached them with a few men, and this dispersed them entirely. I know of no more bloody or heroic fight on record—where great coolness, with the most lion-like courage, saved a few men from slaughter. My father has often told me, that his father considered that the greatest danger he ever encountered, and that he was determined to live and die on the spot, where he had with 25 men beat fairly 185 picked warriors in a battle that was as bloody as ever recorded for the number engaged. The Indians ever afterwards called him "Ski-a-gus-ta," which signifies "Great Warrior," and to his death they called him nothing else. The great McGillivray, afterwards chief of the Creek Nation, wrote him a letter by that name, and begged him not to join the Georgians in the war they were then raging against them, and said if he would but keep aloof, he could whip the Georgians on one bank of the Oconee, and raise corn on the other.

Gen. Pickens fought at the battle of Stono and had a horse killed under him there. He captured Brown and his British regulars at the siege of Augusta—and the conquest was complete after the British had held it for years. The militia of Georgia committed some desperate acts after the capture, and tried to kill Brown and his men for their inhuman and brutal conduct in Georgia. And Gen. Pickens placed Brown and some men in a boat, with a company of men to guard them, and sent them down the river to Savannah.

Gen. Pickens was also with Lee at Granby—he fought at the siege of Ninety Six, and around it, often; and his brother, a gallant captain of a company, was shot down from the Star Redoubt while he was at the entrance of the mine that was digging by the Whigs to blow the fort up. Another brother was there captured by the Tories, and put into the hands of the Indians, and afterwards taken across Savannah river, and burnt by the Indians and some Tories on a pile of lightwood erected in what is now Columbia County.

COWPENS.—He commanded all the militia at the Cowpens, and they consisted of the largest portion of the force engaged there. Congress voted him an elegant sword for the battle and a resolution (of thanks), which sword I now have over his portrait in my drawing room, together with the identical sword he fought with on that bloody day. It is a Toledo blade, and bears in Spanish the motto on its blade, "Draw me not without a cause, and sheathe me not without honor."

ENTAW BATTLE.—He afterwards commanded, in conjunction with Gen. Marion, all the militia of N. C. and S. C. at the Entaws, and was struck from his horse by a musket ball which hit him right on his sword buckle, and being dented in saved his life, by making it glance; but it made a deep and permanent hole in his breast, which caused him pain through life. He held his commission entirely from So. Carolina, but always acted cordially with all officers sent out South by Congress and Washington. You know Sumter refused to do this—and this was the reason why Gen. Pickens was in so many general battles, and Sumter in so few except his own.

There is no evidence on record of his (Pickens) ever having received a dollar for his services as an officer, and he is the only officer known of in the State but did receive pay. I got Mr. Black of the Secretary of State's office, who is the best informed man in the State on such points, to search, and he certified to me that Gen. Pickens never drew any pay for his services to the State as an officer. Certificates were given freely by him to enable others to draw pay, but never for himself.

Mrs. Katherine Hunter, Selma, Ala., is the youngest and only surviving child of Gen. Pickens—a widow.

He was appointed to command by Gen. Washington after the war in an expedition against the Northwestern Indians, but declined. And he was appointed by Jefferson and others to hold various treaties, and run boundary lines between N. C. and Tennessee.—End.

MAJ. JOHN BOWIE.—Was born 10th May, 1740, in the Parish of New Kirkpatrick, Dumbartonshire, Scotland. He immigrated to America in 1762 and landed in Va. June 8th of that year. His first business was carrying on a traffic with the Cherokee Indians in that portion of their country which is now called Tennessee. July 28, 1767, he married Rosa Reid, daughter of Col. George Reid, when he abandoned his traffic with the Indians, and settled on Long Cane Creek, where he continued to reside until his death, Sept. 20, 1827.

On the 25th Feb., 1776, he was commissioned a captain in the 5th regiment raised by S. C., and soon after put on Continental establishment. In March, 1777, his company, with another belonging to the same regiment, was by resolution of the Governor and Council detached from the 5th regiment and made Independent Companies in the service of the State. He participated in the battle of Stono, and at the storming of Savannah, in both of which he acted as Brigade Major. In the battle of Guilford having no command, he acted as a volunteer extra aid to Gen. Huger, the second in command. At the period of the battle of Entaws he was sick in a hospital, and unable to participate. After the war of the Revolution, he was for a number of years clerk for the County Court for Abbeville County.

The above, says Alexr. Bowie, in a letter to Robt. H. Wardlaw, is from my memorandum book to which it was transferred from his own lips several years before his death.

COL. JAMES SYLES.—Chas W. Hodges writes to Dr. Logan, Maybinton, June 11, 1858, that Mrs. Elizabeth Maybin of that place, in her 77th year, says, her paternal grandfather, Ephraim Syles, was the first settler in that part of Fairfield Co. near Syles' Ford—that he came from N. C., and died before the war. Her father was James Syles, was actively engaged in the war; he was taken prisoner by the British and Tories, and died in Chester District of small-pox.

GEN. PICKENS.—Andrew W. Shilleto writes: Abbeville, Aug. 20, 1857; Gen. Pickens' old neighbor who he kicked a little was one of King George's most loyal subjects, and he made it his especial business, so soon as he heard of any victory the British had gained, or any advantage the British or Tories had got of the rebels, as he called the Whigs, he could not be easy until he had told his news at Gen. Pickens' and John White's. What news he had to tell the day of the kicking I do not remember; but the General happened to be at home, and as soon as the old fellow got through with his good news, he began to boast of his King, of the discipline and bravery of his army, and said that King George had never been conquered—that it was in vain for the rebels to contend with him, for they would "be kilt." The General could not listen to him any longer; he rose up, took the old fellow by the hand, led him to the gate, and kicked him down the hill to the block house branch, some hundred and thirty or forty yards."

COL. JOHN WILLIAMS, of N. C., son of Daniel and Ursula Williams, was born in November, 1737; his brother Col. John Williams (of King's Mountain) in November, 1740; Joseph Williams, September, 1742—and four other children. From family record; John W. became a judge in N. C.

"Once," says Col. John D. Williams, "Bill Cunningham rode up to one Neely's, a Tory, residing on the opposite side of Little river from Col. Jas. Williams, and asked if Col. W. was at home? "Yes," said Neely. "Well, give me some dinner as soon as you can, for I shall go over and kill him this evening." Neely's daughter, a young lady, heard him, and slipping quietly off, crossed the river, and apprised Col. Williams of Cunningham's design. He mounted his horse, and was just riding out of his avenue, when Cunningham came in sight, and gave chase, but never overtook him.

After Col. Williams' death—the Tories took possession of the house in which his family resided—and either then forted, or it had been put in that condition by Col. Williams—and Mrs. W. and her six children, three sons and three daughters, the two oldest Daniel and Joseph away in the service, were driven off, and she found shelter in a small school house near the present Little River Church. While living here she was often near perishing, the Tories depriving her even of meal. In the midst of this, the British officers at Ninety Six, hearing of her situation, came to see her, and ordered the Tories to treat her with more humanity. After they (the officers) left, however, they showed the influence of the British over them by burning down her mills on Little River. It was behind the saw pit at this mill, that the Whigs concealed themselves when attacking the fort of Tories around the house.

Col. Williams' parents died in Virginia, when he removed to Carolina (Col. J. D. W. the grandson of the Colonel). Col. Williams' sons, Daniel and Joseph, were respectfully seventeen and thirteen when at King's Mountain; and a year later were slaughtered by Cunningham at Hoyes' Station. John, a younger brother, went (towards the close of the war L. C. D.)

after the war to Va. to keep the negroes from the Tories; and while there took suddenly ill and died—supposed that he was poisoned for money, but he had none—the negroes were saved to the family.

"My mother often said that Cunningham would come and take out the family, even her father, Rich. Griffin, and whip them to make them tell where the Whigs were hid. They often too robbed their house of whatever they could get. Had to hide out their money.

The family came from Orange (Hanover) County, Virginia. He married a Clarke.

When Cunningham had selected Col. Hayes and Daniel Williams to be hung, on the fodder-stack pole, Joseph Williams said, "Brother, what shall I tell mother when I go home?" "You d—d young rebel, you shall tell her nothing," and instantly cut him down. The two surviving sons, James and Washington—former died about 1835—latter in 1827—and latter father of Col. John D. Williams, and Mrs. ——.

THE RING FIGHT.—Miss Susan Long's tradition says:

In the Ring Fight in the Indian nation a young man named Thomas Ellison was one of the participants—from Duncan's creek—he was of great muscular strength, and sustained a desperate hand-to-hand struggle with a powerful Indian. The Indian, it seems, was so oily, that Ellison could get no hold of him, while Ellison having very long hair, the Indian had a great advantage of him. Ellison lost his knife in the struggle, but after a great effort he got the Indian's who gave up at once, when Ellison killed and scalped him. He was astonished when he looked up to find the whites victorious, help having just come up.

On one occasion (says Miss Susan Long) Col. Nixon and Col. Joseph Hayes (of Hayes Station) attacked a station of Tories in a house on the Tyger, in the lower part of Union. Nixon was shot down as they approached the house. Hayes rushed to the door, and by means of a rail broke it down, and had got some distance into the building, when looking back he found himself deserted by his men. He then fought his way out, and made his escape. Nixon was shot in the back and lived till next day, lying where he had fallen. No Whig dared to go to his help for fear of the sharp-shooters in the house. It was said that a hundred dollars were offered any man who would bring him off. When Hayes was pushing in the door, the lady of the house rushed out by him, doubtless a Tory, but frightened, and after running some distance from the building received a ball shot by one of the Tories—whether by accident or design, is not known. Her screams moved the sympathies of the Whigs, and they intimated to the Tories that they could send out and remove her to the house; they did so,—whether she survived was never ascertained. The Whigs had divided into four companies as they attacked the house—Hayes burst open the door with a rail—Nixon was shot from a window. They had to abandon the siege.

COL. SAM HAMMOND.—Miss Susan Long, daughter of Robt. Long (of Abbeville)—says: "It was on this same plantation that Robert Long, in a deep ravine that runs up from Miller's creek, concealed and fed—Hammond, and a Whig from Georgia, till having induced some 14 or 15 Whigs to join him, and whom he (Long) led to the ravine at night, when he sallied out. In after years Squire Long met Hammond at the State Convention in Columbia, in 1832, when Hammond pointing to Long said to the company at that table, "That man, when a boy of 16 fed me, in Laurens, on Joe Adam's plantation till I was strong enough to venture out in spite of the Tories."

ROBT. IRWIN.—See Ramsay, Tennessee, 129, 131.

MAJ. JOS. WILLIAMS—a cousin of Col. Jos. Williams, killed at King's Mountain—was the youngest son of Nath. Williams, who emigrated from Wales to Hanover County, Va.—Joseph lost his father when he was 15 years old, and was taken care of by a namesake, and kinsman, Jos. Williams, a merchant of Williamsburg, Granville County, N. C. J. Williams settled at the Shallow Ford of Yadkin before the Revolution, and died in Aug., 1827—his widow surviving till 1832. Letter of his son Alexander Williams, Greenville, Tenn., 1845, June 28th. P. S.—I expect I received a letter from the same gentleman you speak of, from Baltimore. Mr. Lyman C. Draper, who wishes to know something of my father, and particularly as to the battle between the Whigs and Tories fought near the Shallow Ford of the Yadkin, at which battle my father headed and commanded the Whigs. It is a little singular, history has never named this battle, although near 100 Tories were killed, and only one Whig lost his life. A. W."

HAMMOND'S STORE, ETC.—"I was at the battle of Hammond's Store. There was a Tory Colonel came from Georgia, and camped there with 400 men or Tories with him, and Bill Cunningham, Mayfield and Pearson came and joined his troops. At that time I was under Morgan at Grindal Shoals. The next morning after we got news, Col. Washington and Col. Hayes with their troops were sent on down there. We marched all that day, and the next day until about 10 o'clock. We made a charge upon them. The battle was not (of long) duration. There were forty Tories killed, and near 200 taken prisoners. Bill Cunningham in making his escape ran a very fine mare to death.

COL. JOS. HAYES succeeded Col. James Williams in command of the regiment. He had previously served as Captain in the regiment.

MAJOR JONATHAN DOWNS received a wound on Williamson's Cherokee campaign. He commanded the fort on Rabun's Creek; he took five Tories there. Major of Williams' regt.

COL. JAMES WILLIAMS was out on the Indian campaign—Williamson's Cherokee expedition. He was at Kettle Creek; at the siege of Savannah he received a spent ball in his forehead—then at Musgrove's Mill—and then at King's Mountain

—mortally wounded, of which he died the next day after the battle at night.

Col. Williams' old place, near what is now Little River Bridge—Col. Hayes, Capt. Simmons, myself and 49 other soldiers, went up near the fort to an old saw-pit, and stopt, at which time Col. Hayes and Capt. Simmons carried a flag into Cunningham, Hayes being well acquainted with him, and introduced Simmons to him, and told him his business. Cunningham desired 3 hours for consideration. Simmons now said it could not be granted. Cunningham then desired 2 hours and a half; Simmons told him he could have only three-fourths of an hour, and at the end of that time he and Hayes would draw up their troops and storm the fort, if not surrendered. They both came back, Simmons looking at his watch to note the time. Near the expiration of the time we discovered them running towards the river—we all charged up to the fort.—Jos. Griffin's statement.

Col. Jos. Hayes and party were massacred 19th Nov. 1781. (*Ms.* letter Col. John Williams, of N. Carolina).

Col. Jos. Williams, in Sept., 1780, by resolution of the General Assembly of N. C., was advanced $25,000 from the State Treasury to be applied in raising troops for the defense of the State. In 1788 his heirs were released from this claim.

Gen. Andrew Pickens.—Capt. John Swelling's statement: George Swelling, my father, was with Gen. Pickens on one occasion when pursuing the Indians up Tugaloo river. Col. Robert Anderson was also with them. The Indians were following them upon one side of the river, while they marched on the other, looking for a convenient crossing place. At length they came to a shoaly place, when Pickens said: "Boys, I think here is a place over which we can cross, and give the enemy a brush." Col. Anderson replied: "But General, those bushes over there are full of Indians." "Yes," said Pickens, "that is just what I want, and if we march thus to the head of the river, there will be just as many in the bushes opposite to the point we may cross—come, boys, follow me!" And plunging in, was received, in the middle of the stream by a shower of balls from the enemy. He said the bullets fell around them in the water like muscadines from overhanging vines, and yet not a man was hurt. By the time the corps reached the opposite bank, not an Indian was to be found.

BATTLE OF CEDAR SPRING.—In the Carolina Cpartan, Spartanburg, Aug. 2, 1855, is an account of a celebration at Cedar Springs, July 25th preceding, at which Hon. J. Winsmith delivered an appropriate address from the historical portion of which, the following extracts are made: After mentioning that Rawdon soon after the fall of Charleston was sent to Camden, and Cruger to Cambridge or Ninety Six—

"And in accordance with the policy of the British, after what they considered the general submission of the State, to increase the royal force by embodying the people of the country as a British militia, Major Ferguson, a brave and distinguished officer, was sent to the upper districts to train the most loyal inhabitants, and attach them to the corps. Ferguson encountered no opposition, and was quite successful for some time in the objects of his mission, and even until he entered the lower part of Spartanburg District.

"About this time Col. Sumter whose name, in connection with our Revolutionary struggle, cannot fail to excite in the breast of every Carolinian the warmest emotions of admiration and gratitude, had at the head of a little band of freemen, returned to his own State. About the same time, too, Major Clarke, of Georgia, who had been repulsed in an attack upon Augusta, marched through the upper part of South Carolina to join Sumter, then near the Catawba, in York District.

"Colonel Sumter, impressed with the importance of making some show of resistance to the heretofore unimpeded progress of Ferguson, whose mission had thus far proved a triumphal march, requested Major Clarke to take his Georgia troops, and an additional force which he proposed to furnish, and move over into Spartanburg district, for the purpose of annoying Ferguson—hoping that it would, at least, have the effect to revive the drooping spirits of those who were favorably disposed to the Whig cause.

"In accordance with this arrangement, Clark crossed Broad river, and somewhere in his march towards Ferguson, was unexpectedly joined by Cols. McDowell and Shelby with a few men. After McDowell and Shelby joined him it was determined that, as the expedition had been entrusted to Clarke, he should still retain the command.

"Ferguson was informed of this movement before Clark approached very near him, and determined at once to force him to make a precipitate retreat or fight. And as Clarke's command was far inferior to that of the enemy, badly equipped and provided for in every way, prudence compelled him to retreat. In his retreat he encamped for the night somewhere near Fairforest Creek, and about two miles from this place. Before day, the spies came in, and gave the information that Ferguson was within half a mile of them. Clarke immediately resumed his retreat, and Ferguson coming up to his encampment, and finding that he had left, immediately detached Capt. Dunlap, with about sixty British dragoons, and one hundred and fifty or sixty volunteer mounted riflemen in pursuit, with orders to overtake Clarke, and engage him until he could bring up his whole force.

Some where near this place—just on yon hill, as I have always understood it—the spies came running in, and informed Clarke that Ferguson's horse were in sight. Clarke, with the approbation of his whole command, immediately determined to fight; and consequently formed, and waited to receive them. Dunlap's volunteer mounted riflemen, who were in front, recoiled and gave back at the first fire of their opponents, and Dunlap found it difficult to rally them. Having done so, however, he placed himself at the head of his dragoons, and led them on, followed by the mounted riflemen, to a bold and spirited attack. For a while it was a fierce contest; but Dunlap having lost about half of his dragoons, and the volunteer riflemen not appearing much disposed to come into very close quarters, he was compelled to retreat, and he was pursued with great vigor and spirit until he met Ferguson, who had put his whole force in motion to relieve him.

"Clarke, with his small band, being unable to oppose the whole force of Ferguson, was now compelled to retreat. And perhaps in that retreat he displayed equal courage, and more skill, than was exhibited in any part of the engagement; for having captured about twenty British dragoons and several volunteer riflemen, his retreat was consequently much retarded by the attention necessary for their security; and as the dragoons were the choice troops of Ferguson's command, he felt and avowed a determination to recapture them and taking the command himself, he pressed so hard on Major Clarke's retreat, that in order to secure his prisoners, he was compelled to skirmish with his pursuers from every favorable position between this place and what was then known as the old Iron Works, now Bivingsville. Leaving some wounded soldiers at the old Iron Works, Major Clarke was enabled to hasten his retreat; and Ferguson, finding it unavailing, desisted from further pursuit.

"I have thus given you, fellow citizens, what I consider a correct account of the Battle of Cedar Spring. I have, with much care and considerable labor, examined all the published statements upon the subject, and find them materially different. In some of them it was stated that the battle was fought before day at Clarke's camp, and no notice is taken of the presence of either McDowell or Shelby on the occasion. But the Biography of General Shelby, published in the National Portrait Gallery, states that Colonel Shelby had the command in the battle at this place, and that he had six hundred men. Thus it will be seen how different and contradictory are the published statements upon the subject.

All the accounts concur in establishing the conclusion that our little Revolutionary band earned for themselves, on this occasion, the reputation of patriot soldiers. Not a man gave way. Every one performed the part assigned him with promtitude and spirit. Major Clarke was a distinguished officer and brave man, and on this occasion he commanded with great skill, and fought with a daring courage, amounting almost to rashness. And the biographer of General Shelby says that he had often heard Shelby mention the circumstance of his stepping in the midst of battle to look with admiration and astonishment at Clarke fight! And I know, fellow citizens, that I express less than you feel, when on this occasion I offer to his memory, in your behalf and for myself, the tribute of our most grateful acknowledgements.

There is no allusion whatever to the tradition of Mrs. Dillard or Mrs. Thomas giving information of the British approach.

INDEX

LOGAN MANUSCRIPT
Prepared by

Colleen Morse Elliott
Fort Worth, Texas

......., Bettie/Betty
 (Indian) 17
Catawba George (Indian)15
Jackson (Indian) 17
King Hagler (Indian) 16
McGillivray (Indian) 105
Monday (Indian) 51
New River (Indian) 15
Old Dick (African) 103,104
Old Scott (Indian) 15
Paul (Negro) 33
Ski-a-gus-ta 105
Sky-gusta 49,50,51
Virginia Poll 56
Virginia Sal 7

Adair, John 62,63
 Wm. 62,63
Adams, Joe 111
Adamson...62,63
Alexander...46,87
 Joseph 36
Allen, Chas. H. 94,97
Allison, Robt. 64
 Robt. T. 64
Alston...95
Anderson...77,103,104
 Mary 49,50,51
 Robert 49,50,51,113

Ball, Isaac 63
 John M. N. 63
Barksdale...8
Barnett, Humphrey 64
 Jacob 64
Barnwell...15
Beal, Wm. 51,52,53
Beard, James 77
Beatie, David 67
Beckham, John 38,39
Beggs, Anna 57
Berry, Wm. 91
Black...107
 James A. 101
 Jane 44
 Thom./Tom 63,64
 Wm. 69
Blackstock...33,91
 Mary 60
 Wm. 60
Blasangam/Blassengam 4,5
Bobo...75
 E. M. 79
Bogan...46.47
Boone, Daniel 39,45
Bowen, Reece 67
Bowie...3
 Alex'r 108
 John 107
 Rosa 107
Bowles, Isabella 34
Bowrie, Alexander 69
Boyd...2,48,102
Braddock...46,98
Brandon...4,5,34,57,58,67,
 Ann 58
 Benj. 47
 C. 49
 Elizabeth 43,58
 George 47
 James 58
 Jane 58
 John 47
 Thomas 2,43,47,58
 William 58

Bratton...4,7,62,63,73,86
 Hugh 91
 Mrs. J. S. 61
 Robert 61
 Tom 63
 Wm. 8,61,63,82,91
Brown...2,58,92,106
Bryan...87
Buchanan...23
 John 22
Buford...83
Bull...16
Burgess...9
Butler, Wm. 9,101

Caldwell...18
 Galbraith 64
 John 57
Calhoun...98,99
 Agnes 54
 E. R. 1
 Ezekiel 54,94,95,97
 James 54,97,98
 J. C. 97
 John E. 1
 Nancy 54
 Pat/Patrick 8,54,94,97
 William/Wm. 8,54,94,97
Cameron...3
 Alexander 60
Campbell...10,53,55,56,61
 B. R. 8
 David 66
 Robert 64,66,67
 Wm. 65
Carnes...32
 P. 31
Carr...56
 Paddy 80,100
 Wm. 91
Carroll, John 61,82
 Joseph 82
 Thomas 82
Carrouth, Mary 50
Carson, Wm. 8
Carter...45
Casey...4,5
 Levi 1,6,7
Cates...66
Chambers...64
Chronicle...9,69
Clark(e)...2,102,110,114,
 115,116,117
 John 10,11
 Elijah 48
Clendenen/Clendennen 62
 Tom 61
 Wm. 63
Cleveland...54,60,66,95
Clinton...82
 Joseph 88
 Peter 88
Clowney...33
 Samuel 32,58
 Wm. K. 59
Coffee, Sale 83
Colvill, Andrew 67
Cook, Eli 35,37
Cornels...104,105
Cornwallis...18,27,35,87,
 91,96,101
Corry, James 67
Cowley, Robert 84
Crabtree, Wm. 67
Crafton, Benj. 1

Crawford...69
 Enos 76,77
 James 68,78
 John 77,78
 Peggy 78
 Robert 68
Creig, Robert 67
Croman, West 77
Crosby, Nancy 79
 Polly 72
Crow, James 68
Cruger...31,74,79,89,114
Cue, John D. 1
Culbertson, Josiah 45
 Martha 45
Cunningham...12,36,78,109,
 110,112,113
 "Bloody" Bill 51,52,53,
 54,112
 Will 5,7
Curry, Nicholas 92

Dansby, Daniel 29
 Martha 19
Davidson...101
Davie...72
Davis, Warren R. 88
Dawkins, E. 92
 Nancy 92
Dennis, John 63
Dickson, Wm. 8
Dillard...74,117
 James 1,3,6,7,13,14
Dooley...102
Dow, Lorenzo 81
Downes...64
Downs, Jonathan 53,112
Draper, Lyman C. 112
Dryden, Nathaniel 67
Dugan...4,12
 Thomas/Thos. 1,7
Dunlap...115
 Wm. 32,53
Dysart, James 67

East, Bethiah S. 54
Easterwood...38,39
Edmondson, Andrew 67
 Robert 67
 William 67
Ellet...34
Ellis...47
Ellison, Thomas 110
Ewing...4,5,6,7,13

Fair...4
Farr...43
 Wm. 45
Farrow, Jane 81
 John 81
 Landon 81
 Mary 81
 Patillo 89
 Rosa 81
 Samuel 81,82
 Sarah 81
 Thomas 81,82,89
Feemster, James 64
 John 64
Ferguson...7,10,55,56,65,
 69,75,99,114,115,116
 Hank 8
Ferris...90
Fincher...79
Finley...77

Finsley...34,82
  Golding 33
Fletchfall, Thomas 44
Ford, John 89
Foster...32,33

Garden...103
Gaston...72
Gates...75
Geiger, Harmon 49
George...35,81
Gill, John 91
  Mary 91
Gillam, Robert 3
  Robert C. 9
Gist, Mrs. S. 44
Glover...9
Golding, Richard 1
Gondelock, David 36
Goodwin...2
  Chamberlain 57
  Charles 57
  Eliza 57
Gordon, George 75
Goudy...98
Gouldelock, Adam 92
  Sallie 92
Graham...10
Gray...57
  James 99,100
  Wm. 53
Green(e)...1,12,20,57,96,101
Greer, Isaac 13
  J. 2
  Joseph 3
  Josiah 1
Gregory, Freelove 36
Griffin, Jos. 54,55,113
  Rich. 110
Guist, Nathaniel 67

Hambright...56
Hames, James, Sr. 67
Hamilton...48,95
Hammond...2,112
  LeRoy 31,101
  Sam'l 13,31,90,111
Hampton...90
  John 22
Hamright...8
Hanes, Sam'l 38
Hannah, Robert 78,82
Harris...4,5
  A. T. 51
  John 51
  Mary 51
  Robt. A., Jr. 69
Harrison...21
  Reuben 20,29
Hatchford, John 82
Hauk...8,61,62,63,91
Hayes...4,5,7,110,111,112
  J./Jo. 6,13
  Jos./Joseph 3,12,54,110,112,113
Henderson...21,29,67,82
  Eliza 38
  John 93
  Wm. 38,93
Henry, Robert 9,10
Hill...54,63,86,87
  Wm. 82,90
Hillhouse, John 91
  Wm. 84,86,91
Hodge, Moses 39
Hodge(s), Wm. 38,39
Hodges, Chas. W. 108
Holmes...65
Hood...84,85
  Mary 85
Hopkins...47,72
Houston...97

Houston, John 2
Howard...13,96
Howe...8
  Robert 2
Huger...70,108
Hughes, Joseph 40,41,42,43,44
  Richard 46
  R. W. 40,43
  Sarah 44
  Wm. 44,46
Humphreys, D. 49
Hunter...38
  Katherine 107
Hutchinson...20
  Betty 68
  Grace 68
  Jinny 68
  Molly 68
  Peggy 68
  Sally 68
Hutton, John N. 54
  Jos. 54
  Nancy 54

Inman...13,74,76
Innis...74,79
Irwin, Alex'r/Alexander 9,94
  Ann 94
  Elizabeth 94
  Francis 94
  James 94
  John 9,60,69,94
  Margaret 94
  Mary 60,94
  Robert 9,60,69,93,94,111
  Samuel 9,94
  Sarah 94
  Wm. 60,93,94
Isham...29

Jackson, Andrew 68
  James 6,103
James...9
Jameson, Joseph 84
Jamieson...47
Jamieson/Jamison, James 64,86
  John 64
Jefferies, John 49
Jefferson...27
Jeter, Mrs. M. 46
Johnson...35
  Dick 31
Johnston, James 19
Jolly...36,37
  Benjamin 44,47
  John 44,47
  Joseph 44
  Sarah 47
Jones, John 7
Junes...20

Kennedy, John B. 59
  W. 47
Kilgore, Benj. 1,89

Lacey...4,10,12,31,54,63
Laird, James 67
Lantrip...4
Lee...34
  Amos 49
  Bill 35,36
  Wm. 59
Leonard, Lockley 1
Leslie, John 68
  Samuel 68
Liddle/Liddel...49
  Jared 76
Little, James 48,49
Linch...77

Logan, J. H. 9
  John H. 1
Long, Agnes 8,54
  D. C. 14
  Robert 1,12,13,14,111
  Susan 110,111
Lowe, Andrew 82
Lusk, James 45
  Letitia 45
Lyle...2
Lyon, Humberson 67

McCamie(McKemey), George 68
McClure...8,63
  David 78
  James 78
  John 61
McColloch, Thomas 67
McCool, Elizabeth 43
  Jane 45
  John 86
  Jos. 45
McCord...8
McCrery...2
  Matthew 1
  R. 3
  Robert 1
McDaniel(s)...34,36,37,46
McDowell...6,66,115
McElwee, Isaac 64
  James 64
  John 64
  William 64
McFunkin...36,37
  Ann 45
  Daniel 40,47,48
  Jos./Joseph 43,45,47,49
  Sam'l 46,47
McGowen, Samuel 64
McIlwaine, James 45
McLure, E. C. 10
McNees, Jas. 1
McWhorter, Shelton 39

Mabry, Jack 41,42
Marion...67,68,106
Marshall, J. H. 101
Martin, James 90
Mathis, Drury 55
Maxwell, Mary 50
May, Benjamin 17,29
Maybin, Elizabeth 108
Mayfield,...83,112
Mayson, James 32
Means, G. W. 32
Meek...84,85
  Adam 64
  Edward 85
  James 64
  Moses 64
Meng, Garland 40
Mercer...97
Miles, L. 33
Miller...79
  John 90
Milling, John 18
Mills, John 18,91
  Mary 91
Milner, Wm. 3
Moffett, John 82
Money...19,33
Moore...5,12
  Gum-Log 63
  Henry 23
  James 63
  John 61,63
  John, Jr. 62
  John S. 85
  Maurice 63
  M. D. 54
  Patrick 46
  Philander 63

Moore, Sam 60
  Starr 61,63,64
  Wm. 63
Morgan...5,6,7,13,96,112
Moseley, James 39,40
Mucklerath...21
Murray, Sallie 92
Musgrove(s), Beaks 37,80
  Edward 73,75,79
  Hannah 79
  Leah 79
  Lenny (Lena) 79
  Margaret 75,79
  Mary 79,80,81
  Nancy 79
  Rachel 79
  Sarah 81
  Susan 79
  William 79
Myddelton...90

Neal...82
  Andrew 86,87
Neely, George 3
Neil, William 67
Newell, Samuel 67
Nixon...4,110,111
Noble...3,97
Norris...94,97
Nott, Angelica 49

Odle, John 13
O'Neall...31
Otterson...91
  James 46
  S./Sam 35,40,46,59

Palmer...2
  Sarah 47
Parker...97
  Peter 25
Parsons...89
Patterson...99
Pearson...21,24,31,112
  John 23
  Philip 20
  Philip Edward 14
Pendleton...9
Pickens...2,7,13,15,34,35,
  49,67,68,70,71,76,104,
  105,106,108
  A. 5,6
  Andrew 3,50,51,77,94,
  113
  F. W. 94,97,101
  John 77
  Joseph 77,105
  Joshua 3
  Mary 50,51
Pickett...96
Pinckney...60
Pitt...69
Porter, Alexander 76
  Hugh 76,77
Prevost...26
Prince...69
Probert...9
Pucket, Mary 81
Purves...1
Purvis, John 32

Radcliff...42
Rainey, Sam 63
Ramsey...15
  David 57
  Ephraim 57
  Mary Ann 57
  Richard 57
  Sallie 57
Randall, Jacob 56
  Silas 56
Rapley...71
Rawdon...20,31,57,114

Ray, Henry 84
Reed...94
Reid, George 107
  James 84,86
  Rosa 107
Retter...64
Rhett...15
Richardson...12
Ritchey, Robert 1
Roberson, Joe 84
Roberts...64
Robertson...7
  Watty 18
  William 99
Robinson(Robertson), Horse
  Shoe 60,79,86
  Joseph 83
Roebuck...5,6
  Benjamin 45,89
  George 89
Rogers, James 46
  John 46
Ross...79
  Frank 90
  John 59
  Robert 3
Rosser, Wm. 8
Rowells...64
Russell, Wm. 67
Rutledge...21

Saddler, David 61,63
  Richard 63
Salvadore...23
Salvador...65
  Francis 64
Sapold...92
Saxon, Charles 3
  Hugh 3
Saye...49
  James H. 43
Scaife...43
Scott...58
Senf...30
  John Christian 29
Sevier...53,54
Shaw, Alexander 59
Shearer...64
Shelby...10,53,54,73,115
Shellito, Andrew (W.) 76,
  108
Sherer...4
Simmons...113
Simonton, John 8
Simpson, John 63
Sims, Mrs. C. 40
  Charles 34,35,38,46
  Clough S. 46
  I. S. 91
  Isabella 34
  James S. 46
  Knight 34,46
  Matthew 34
  S. T. 34
  Star 38
  William/Wm. 34,36,37,
  40,46,49
Smart...63
Smith...8,77
  Aaron 64
  Charles 1
  E. P. 89
  Isaac 89
  Jared 6,7
  John 13
  J. Winn 89
  Ralph 89
  Sam'l 49
  Wm. 45,89
  Wm. Eliphas 89
Starke...32
  Robert 31
Starr...63

Steen...46
  James 43
Stevens...3
Stidham, Adam 57
Sumpter, Thomas 3
Sumter/Sumpter 4,13,17,18,
  19,20,27,38,81,82,84,
  85,86,87,90,91,92,101,
  106,114
  Tom 19
Swain...103
Swelling, George 113
  John 113
Swing, Sam'l 3
Syles...60
  Anomanos 31
  Ephraim 108
  James 31,108
  W. 30

Tarleton...4,5,6,13,38,39,
  83,91,92,96,102,103
Taylor, Eliza 38
  Simon 38
  Thomas/Tom 8,38,39
Thomas...2,5,6,95,117
  Abraham 45
  Ann 45
  Jane 44,45
  John 44,45,89,90
  Letitia 45
  Martha 45
  Robert 45
  Wm. 45
Thompson...46,49
Thomson...15
  Matthew 76
  Wm. 29
Thurston, James 29
Trible...77
Triplet...6
Turnbull...18
Turner...24
  Ned 10,11
  Sam 64
Tutt, Eliza 57
  Henry 57
Tyles...4

Van Binkel...30
Vernon, T. O. P. 9

Walker...10
  Agnes Keller 57
  Eliza 57
  Mary Ann 57
Walkup, S. H. 68
Wallace, Leroy Joseph 90
  Wm. 90
Wardlaw, James 60
  Robt. H. 108
Washington...5,6,12,21,20,
  112
  Will 19
Waters...34
  B./Boardwine 10,11,12
  Laudon 10,11
  Margaret 75
  Phil. 10,11,12
  Philemon 75,81
  P. M. 11,73,79
Watson...4
Weir, Thos. 14
Weyniss...8
White...42,45
  Andrew 76,77,78
  John 108
Williams...4,5,10,12,54,56,
  73,113
  Alexander 112
  J. 3
  Daniel 109,110
  James/Jas. 1,31,89,109,

Williams, James (cont'd):
  110,112
  John 2,109,113
  John D. 109,110
  Joseph 109,110,111,112,
    113
  Nath. 111
  Ursula 109
  Washington 110
Williamson...2,12,15,22,
  23,32,43,62,65,72,73,
  98
  A. 1,3
  Andrew 57,70,71
  Annie 57
  James 61,63
  Lauder 61
  Mary Ann 57
  Samuel 61,63
Willison...31
Wilson, David 8
  John 88
  Robert 83,84,86,88
Winn...25,26,28,63
  John 2
  Rhd./Richard 8,24
Winsmith...41
  J. 51,114
Woodward...20,25
  Thos. 28
Wren...68
Wright...2
  Sarah 44

Young, J. 43
  John 58
  Polly 58
  Thomas/Thos. 47,49,57,
    58,59

PLACE NAME INDEX:

Abbeville 78
Albemarle co., Va. 46
Alligator Swamp 2
Allison's Creek 82
Altamaha 2
Antrim, Ireland 7
Antriver country, Ireland
  1
Beach Island 57
Beaufort District 22
Beaufort Island 23
Berkshire, England 23
Bersheba Church 85
Bethel Church 50
Bethel Congregation 88
Bethesda 63
Biggin Church 85
Big Shoemake (Creek Nation)
  3
Bivingsville 116
Blackstock's Battle 12,13,
  19,43,48
Blairsville, S. C. 88
Briar Creek Battle 85,88
Brown's Battery 2
Brown's Creek 43
Brown's Creek Presbyterian
  Church 47,58,59
Brushfort 5
Buffenton's Iron Works 4
Bullock's Creek 86
Bullock's Creek Church 42
Bush River Church 11
Caife's Ferry 41
Calhoun's Mills 94
Cambridge 53
Camden Ferry 30
Cane Creek Church 46
Catawba Creek, Bottetourt
  co., Va. 15
Cat Head Swamp 2
Cedar Shoal 81

Cedar Spring Battle 32,
  33,114
Cedar Springs Church 76
Changee Creek 60
Cherokee Ford Road 56
Clap's Ferry 20
Clarke's Ford 85
Clem's Branch 86
Cook's Mills 59
Cowpens 5,13,34,42,43,102,
  103,106
Craven co., S. C. 14
Cross Creek Battle 60,89
Crowder's Creek 83
Cumberland co., Pa. 46
Cuthay's Plantation 66
Deny 19
De Witt's Corner 64,65
Duck River, Tenn. 28
Dunkin's Creek 4,13
Dutch Ford 11
Enoree (Spartanburg) 2
Entaw Battle 31,106
Entaw Springs 12,38,85
Erskine College 64
Esseneca 65
Fairfield, S. C. 17,22
Fairforest 5,9
Ferguson's Markee 7,8
Fish Dam Ford 8,45,72,79
Fishing Creek 62,63,85
Fishing Creek Church 63
Fort Barrington 25
Fort Granby 67
Fort Motte 8
Fort Moultrie 15
Fort St. Illa 25
Gilbert Town 6,53,100
Glenn's Spring 32
Gossett's Mills 59
Greenville, Tenn. 112
Grindal's Shoals 5,38,39,
  40,48,92
Grave's Ford 20
Guilford 69,96
Hacolalor 94
Haddell's Point 83
Hagler's Branch 85
Hamilton's Ford 92
Hanging Rock 27,31,43,72,
  82
Hannah Hill 82
Hard Labor Creek 98
Harmony Church 84
Haye's Station 32
Head's Ford 81
High Hills 38,39
Hill's Iron Works 4,63
Hobkirk Hill 20
Hogskin Creek 65
Holanswith's Mill 4
Hopewell 50
Hopewell Church 94
Horn Lake, Miss. 59
Howell's Ferry 91
Hoye's Station 109
Ingleman's Mill 20
Jacksonboro 47
Jone's Ford 74
Kelso's Creek 33
Kettle Creek Battle 102
King's Mountain 53,54,55,
  64,99,100
Langley's Fort 65
Laurens Dist., S. C. 1
Lee's Creek 18
Lewis's Turn Out 62
Lexington Dist., S. C. 22
Lindley's Fort 12
Little River 1,2
Little River Church 109
Lochaber 60
Lockhart Shoals 83
Long Cane Bridge 94

Long Cane Church 50
Love's Ford 4
McCool's Ferry 41,43,44
McCord's Creek 77
Matagorda, Texas 14
Mecklenburg, Va. 67
Mobley's Meeting House 17
Musgrove's Mill 10,11,13,
  33,34,43,60,73,79,81
Nation Ford 85
New Kirkpatrick, Scotland
  107
Oconee Mountain 65
Ogle's Mills 32
Old Bethany 64
Otterson's Fort 59
Picken's Block House 76,
  94,95,96,104
Piney Woods House 1
Quaker Church 35
Ransom's Mill 6
Rocky Mount 18,30,43,82
Saluda Old Town 55
Sandy River Settlement 72
Scaife's(Scaufe's)Ferry
  43,44
Scheerer's Ferry 20
Sherard's Ford 6
Sherer's Ferry 4
Skal Shoal 5
Spring Hill 35
Stone Church 50
Strother's Ferry 20
Syle's Ford 108
Therer's Ferry 13
Tobler's Fort 54
Tyger Fair 4
Walker's Cross Road 8,62
Waxhaw Bridge 69
White Hall 64,70,98
White's Mills 91
Young's Mill 32

www.ingramcontent.com/pod-product-compliance
Lightning Source LLC
Chambersburg PA
CBHW020657300426
44112CB00007B/421